# Devoted

## Steps of Love
## Toward Healthy Relationships

## ALSO BY BRENDA PACE

*Journey of a Military Wife*

> *Dedicated: Steps of Faith in God's Plan*
> *Devoted: Steps of Love Toward Healthy Relationships*
> *Deployed: Steps of Hope in Times of Uncertainty*
> *Directed: Steps of Peace in Times of Transition*

*Medals Above My Heart: The Rewards of Being a Military Wife*
*(Coauthored with Carol McGlothlin)*

*The One Year Yellow Ribbon Devotional: Take a Stand*
*in Prayer for Our Nation and Those Who Serve*
*(Coauthored with Carol McGlothlin)*

# Devoted

## Steps of Love
## Toward Healthy Relationships

# BRENDA PACE

 AMERICAN BIBLE SOCIETY

Philadelphia

DEVOTED: STEPS OF LOVE TOWARD HEALTHY RELATIONSHIPS
(JOURNEY OF A MILITARY WIFE SERIES)

By Brenda Pace
Edited by Peter Edman, Davina McDonald, and Stacey Wright

© 2016 American Bible Society

ISBN 978-1-941448-58-8
ABS Item 124539

Design by Jordan Grove
Cover image by Joshua Wann

Set in Arno Pro and Avenir

American Bible Society
101 North Independence Mall East
Philadelphia, PA 19106

www.american.bible

Printed in the United States of America

# Contents

---

An online version of JOURNEY OF A MILITARY WIFE is also available. You can find this book series, small group study guides, and a place to invite others to share this journey with you at www.MilitaryWife.bible.

# Journey 1

*Devoted to My Husband*

# Introduction

The military lives by an old axiom: "Recruit the Soldier (Sailor/Airman/Marine), Retain the Family." It is, in part, a reminder that what motivates a person to join the military may not be what motivates him or her to stay. When it comes to marriage, attraction and passion can lead a couple to the altar to say "I do," but it is commitment and devotion that will keep them together on the journey "till death us do part."

Every marriage, not just military marriages, needs to draw on positive relationship attributes to grow strong. But military couples have to be creative in how best to relate to each other during times of separation and duty. In marriage, a wife looks beyond what is good only for her and focuses on what is good for her husband—and what is best for their marriage.

Each day, you will find a devotional waypoint. A *waypoint* is a stopping place on a journey. It is a single specific location. Waypoints may be places where you want to return, or they may be a significant landmark. During this thirty-day journey in the Scriptures, we will visit important waypoints of intimacy, trust, extended family, stewardship, and marital roles. Over the years, strong and healthy marriages make frequent stops at these waypoints. Regardless of how long you have been traveling with your husband, a pause for a few moments at these waypoints can refresh you and reenergize your marriage. Before you start each day, pray this prayer from Psalm 119:18: Lord, "Open my eyes, that I may behold wondrous things out of your law."

Why not join with some fellow sojourners to study God's Word together? As a companion to this book you will find online at www.MilitaryWife.bible a set of Bible studies complete with leader and participant notes to guide your discussion.

Enjoy the journey, sister!

# Waypoint 1

*Adam and Eve—traveling toward intimacy*

Read

> Then the LORD God said, "It is not good that the man
> should be alone ..." (Genesis 2:18a)

Reflect

To call my husband "my buddy" sounds a bit trite and corny.
I tend to use that word with little children as a cute term of
endearment. But the military uses *buddy* in a way that brings
depth and purpose. It is anything but cute. In the military, a
buddy can be a means to save a life. The buddy system has come
to represent team cohesion and resilience.

Whether as a shipmate in the Navy or Marines, a wingman
in the Air Force, or a battle buddy in the Army, the military
recognizes the necessity of companionship. Partners are assigned
not just for friendship, but also for physical and emotional
protection. Two buddies watch out for each other and look
after each other's welfare.[1] The military buddy system improves
work performance and is the major source of encouragement
to overcome stressful military-related situations, from basic
training to war zones.[2]

When God created the world, he looked at everything he
created and pronounced it "good." But in Genesis 2:18, God
states emphatically that it is not good for the man to be alone.
In other words, *it is bad*.[3] The contrasting repetition of the word
*good* grabs my attention and highlights the truth that no human
can fulfill God's plan alone—we are made to need a battle
buddy.[4]

The writer of the Old Testament book of Ecclesiastes describes the buddy system poetically:

> Two are better than one, because they have a good reward for their toil. For if they fall, one will lift up his fellow. But woe to him who is alone when he falls and has not another to lift him up! Again, if two lie together, they keep warm; but how can one keep warm alone? And though a man might prevail against one who is alone, two will withstand him—a threefold cord is not quickly broken. (Ecclesiastes 4:9–12)

Life is better and richer when we operate with the buddy system—especially in marriage. We will have greater reward for our work, someone to help us when we fall down, and even someone to keep our feet warm in a cold bed.

### Respond

What positive aspects of the military buddy system can you apply to marriage? How are these characteristics evident in your marriage? Name one characteristic you will focus on this week to strengthen your marriage.

### Prayer for the journey

Lord, thank you for my husband. Strengthen our relationship as we offer love and support to one another. Amen.

# Waypoint 2
## *Made for each other*

"... I will make him a helper fit for him." Now out of the ground the LORD God had formed every beast of the field and every bird of the heavens and brought them to the man to see what he would call them. And whatever the man called every living creature, that was its name. The man gave names to all livestock and to the birds of the heavens and to every beast of the field. But for Adam there was not found a helper fit for him. So the LORD God caused a deep sleep to fall upon the man, and while he slept took one of his ribs and closed up its place with flesh. And the rib that the LORD God had taken from the man he made into a woman and brought her to the man. (Genesis 2:18b–22)

### Reflect

You've seen those couples who look like they were made for each other. It may sound shallow, but be honest—you know exactly what I'm talking about! Scripture does not give us any indication of the appearance of Adam and Eve, but there is no doubt they were made for each other!

The idea conveyed in Genesis 2:18–22 is that God intends to create an indispensable companion for the man.[5] Her contributions would be essential. As his helper, she would do what no one else could. She would not only join in taking care of creation and raising children, but these two would experience the mutual support of companionship.

The animals are presented to the first man Adam for him to name, but none of them pass the implicit test in the *helper fit for him* department. So God provides what is missing, or *who* is missing. God did not make the woman out of dust like man and the animals, but from the very body of the man.

An often-quoted description by the seventeenth-century theologian Matthew Henry communicates the spirit of the text:

> Not made out of his head to top him,
> not out of his feet to be trampled upon by him,
> but out of his side to be equal with him,
> under his arm to be protected,
> and near his heart to be beloved.

Henry's description, though sweet and flowery, is also a glimpse into the ideal of marriage as a relationship marked by harmony and intimacy.[6]

### Respond

Adam and Eve were made for each other. In what ways are you and your husband made for each other?

### Prayer for the journey

Lord, you created me to be in relationship with you and with others. Help the relationship I have with my husband to be one of harmony and intimacy. I know these things do not come naturally, so help me to be willing to do my part. Amen.

# Waypoint 3

*A new family*

Read

> Then the man said, "This at last is bone of my bones and flesh of my flesh; she shall be called Woman, because she was taken out of Man."
>
> Therefore a man shall leave his father and his mother and hold fast to his wife, and they shall become one flesh. (Genesis 2:23–24)

Reflect

"If you want to experience the truth of Genesis 2:24, just marry a soldier, sailor, airman, coastguardsman, or marine. You will then understand to the fullest what God had in mind when he gave the instruction to leave and cleave!" These words from veteran military wife Carol ring true. "Cleave" (the term used in older English translations for this verse) is a word packed with meaning that needs to stick in the minds and hearts of every married couple. In fact, that is exactly the translation of cleave: *to stick with*. The word describes the "inseparable relationship between the man and the woman in marriage as God intended."[7]

Carol recalls the emotions she experienced when, after nine months of marriage, her husband received military orders to Germany. She said, "The idea of going to another country made me think I might never see my parents again." She questioned whether the love she and her husband had for each other would be strong enough to withstand the adjustment of life without her mom and dad.

"Bone of my bones and flesh of my flesh" speaks of the uniting of a husband and wife as one. The wording of Scripture in Genesis 2:24 conveys the radical nature of the marriage union. Consider the case of a female egg and male sperm coming together to form a new human being. One day that new person will physically depart the mother's body and live separately. Though this child shares traits, genes, and relationships with others, the child has an identity apart from the family of origin.

Just as we cut the umbilical cord at the birth of a new baby, there must be a separation from mom and dad so we can *stick with* and *hold fast* to a spouse. A mama wants to hold tight to a newborn baby, but it would be absurd—and unhealthy—for her to want the umbilical cord to remain intact.

Marriage does not mean you forget about your family of origin, but does mean your primary family identity now comes with your spouse. A new union that creates a new family happens when you say, "I do." This union between a man and woman goes beyond physical union toward the union of spirits through love and concern, faithfulness and devotion, support and involvement.[8]

### Respond

What does healthy emotional sustainment look like? What are the dangers of leaning too hard on your husband for emotional sustenance? What other sources of emotional support do you have? How does a military marriage enhance or discourage emotional sustainment?

### Prayer for the journey

Lord, teach me what it means to be *one* with my husband. Give us healthy boundaries, and help us overcome those things that would hinder closeness. Amen.

# Waypoint 4

*More than no clothes*

And the man and his wife were both naked and were not ashamed. (Genesis 2:25)

Intimacy and vulnerability are two words that make me uncomfortable. These words share a strong connection, because in order to be intimate I must be willing to be vulnerable. Imagine a time without vulnerability—but there it is in Genesis 2:25: *"And the man and his wife were both naked and were not ashamed."* Naked. The word alone communicates vulnerability.

Yet at creation Adam and Eve were two completely comfortable and uninhibited sojourners in paradise. *Naked* did not conjure up feelings of body image, insecurity, acceptance, exposure, or exploitation. Naked and unashamed was God's intended plan for marriage. The original state of being for Adam and Eve was intimacy.[9] God provided everything they required and they were content.[10]

God defined the initial concept of intimacy by nakedness, which he characterized by innocence and integrity.[11] Adam and Eve hid nothing from each other. They had no secrets, no agendas, no deception, and therefore no shame. Their nakedness represented openness and trust.[12]

Physical nakedness is a gift for a husband and wife to enjoy together. It is also a metaphor for the emotional and spiritual intimacy of marriage. To disrobe my fears and failures feels risky. What if my husband does not like what he sees in me? Deeper levels of intimacy take time as we erratically remove each layer of concealment until our souls are bare and we are not ashamed.

As the years progress in marriage, two naked bodies will fade from their youthful beauty. But two naked souls can grow into a lovely intimacy that will keep the gleam in the eye 'til death do you part.

### Respond

How would you define emotional intimacy? What are ways you nurture emotional intimacy in your marriage?

### Prayer for the journey

Lord, help the love my husband and I share to grow deeper each day. Protect our relationship and make us willing to be vulnerable, willing to give each other time to bare our souls. Amen.

# Waypoint 5

*An apple a day keeps intimacy away*

Read

> But the serpent said to the woman, "You will not surely die. For God knows that when you eat of it your eyes will be opened, and you will be like God, knowing good and evil." So when the woman saw that the tree was good for food, and that it was a delight to the eyes, and that the tree was to be desired to make one wise, she took of its fruit and ate, and she also gave some to her husband who was with her, and he ate. Then the eyes of both were opened, and they knew that they were naked. And they sewed fig leaves together and made themselves loincloths. (Genesis 3:4–7)

Reflect

A tree at one of my childhood homes was filled with beautiful orange fruit. Our family assumed it was an orange tree and we eagerly awaited the time we could pick the oranges and enjoy fresh juice for breakfast. The day finally came! We plucked the lovely oranges from the tree. We juiced the oranges. We tasted the juice. We all ran for the sink to spit out the vile tasting liquid! The tree deceived us. Its fruit was for ornamentation, not for consumption.

We cannot know what type of fruit Eve and Adam ate in the garden that led to their downfall, but the iconic symbol has become the apple. Like the oranges of my childhood, the fruit looked delicious (and probably was). Moreover, it seemed to hold a special ability to enhance mental faculties that would make one wise. At the urging of the serpent, Eve decided to take a bite and disregard God's warning. Adam, who was with her, wanted to taste the fruit too—and he did.

The act had dire consequences. Eating the fruit ultimately led to their deaths, but the first price recorded in Genesis was the loss of unfettered intimacy as they covered themselves with leaves. Their nakedness was more than skin deep. Disobedience had torn apart a perfect intimacy of souls and wrapped their wounded spirits in the coverings of distorted desire, distrust, blame, and fear.[13]

Since Adam and Eve left the perfect Garden of Eden, couples have had to work hard to rebuild any semblance of their original intimacy. Even in good circumstances, intimacy can take a long time to develop. When we eat the fruit of criticism, distrust, or deceit, intimacy will elude us and we miss a particular purpose God intends for marriage.

Take a lesson from Eve. No matter how tasty a forbidden fruit appears, it doesn't compare with shared intimacy in marriage. Even if one could grant special powers, the results will never match those of following God's plan for an intimate relationship with your husband.

### Respond

What factors can erode intimacy in a military marriage? What factors can improve intimacy in a military marriage?

### Prayer for the journey

Lord, it is easy for me to avoid intimacy. It feels risky and uncomfortable. Don't let me run away from sharing myself completely with my husband. Help me to see the ways that even this military life can help me run toward a deeper connection with him. Amen.

# Waypoint 6

*Joseph and Mary—A journey of trust*

In the sixth month the angel Gabriel was sent from God to a city of Galilee named Nazareth, to a virgin betrothed to a man whose name was Joseph, of the house of David. And the virgin's name was Mary. (Luke 1:26–27)

"Few delights can equal the mere presence of one whom we trust utterly."[14] These words from Scottish novelist and theologian George MacDonald cause me to stop and consider the importance of trust with my husband. Do we share that kind of trust? If so, how did we get to that place?

Just like intimacy, trust is a journey that takes time and is not without risk. I cannot allow my fears to overcome the risk; I must nurture trust. What sort of trust journey makes the risk worthwhile?

Three essential elements of trust are respect, vulnerability, and commitment. We exercise these aspects of trust best in frequent and unhindered interactions with our spouse. But military life usually leads to separations—deployment, training, assignments, and career progression—that can hinder the development of these elements. And the priority of the military mission for every service member can also compete with trust-building in marriage.

The Gospels of Matthew and Luke introduce a young couple that risked a journey into the unknown. Joseph and Mary did not have a military marriage but they certainly faced some unique challenges. Their trust in God—and one another—defined their marital journey. They were willing to risk obedience and in so doing they offer us an exceptional example of trust in marriage even apart from their irreplaceable roles in caring for the Savior of the world. Gossip likely followed this young couple throughout their married life. Yet they trusted God's plan for their lives, which included his plan for their marriage.

Just as a beautiful custom home is built brick by brick, trust in relationships does not come ready made. Relationship expert John Gottman reminds us that a couple builds trust in small moments.[15] Everyday small moments between husband and wife—an encouraging word, a thoughtful deed, a guarded glance, an attentive pause, an honest answer—shape a strong fortress of trust that protects their relationship.

Sisters, building lasting trust takes effort on our part. Often, as with Mary and Joseph, we need intervention from God to shore up the trust factor in our relationships when we exceed our natural human ability. That's a relationship you can trust!

## Respond

What areas of trust do you find are challenged by military marriage? How can you combat these challenges?

## Prayer for the journey

Lord, I pray for small moments of trust-building between my husband and me today. Don't let me miss or waste the moment! Amen.

# Waypoint 7

*Your name is safe*

Read

And her husband Joseph, being a just man and unwilling to put her to shame, resolved to divorce her quietly. (Matthew 1:19)

Reflect

You may have heard the story of the young teacher who asked her class to define love. One child responded, "When someone loves you, your name is safe in their mouth." This well-crafted word picture illustrates how to respect another person. If the story is true, this child has wisdom beyond their years!

Joseph had every reason to think the worst of Mary. He had pledged himself to her, but then she turned up pregnant and he knew he was not the father. In their culture, he could have made a case for her to be stoned to death. No one would have blamed him for criticizing, humiliating, or embarrassing Mary. The law was on his side and he had the right, as well as the expectation, to sever the relationship.[16]

Yet, Mary's name was safe in Joseph's mouth. Matthew informs his readers that Joseph was unwilling to put Mary to shame and instead determined to take care of the situation privately. We can easily admire this man Joseph. Even when he questioned Mary's integrity, he did not degrade her reputation publicly. He displayed both righteousness and kindness by his action to protect Mary's reputation.[17]

With his choice not to shame Mary in public, Joseph paints a powerful portrait of respect. In one of her columns, military wife Julia Plaff includes mutual respect as one of the traits of a successful military marriage. "Successful couples," Plaff explains, "fully appreciate and respect each other. They recognize that the 'jobs' of the military member and the military spouse are difficult and challenging. The sacrifice of one partner is no less important than the sacrifice of the other. Each spouse is committed to the success of the other."[18]

This journey called marriage provides numerous opportunities to exercise respect or disrespect for actions either known or suspected. Follow the example of Joseph and choose to respect your spouse. How safe is his name in your mouth?

### Respond

How do you build trust with your words? Examine the last things you shared about your husband with someone else. How safe would he say his name is in your mouth?

### Prayer for the journey

Lord, I know words are powerful. They have the power of life and death. Help me to speak words of life to and about my husband. *May the words of my mouth and the meditation of my heart be acceptable in your sight, O Lord, my rock and my redeemer.* (Psalm 19:14). Amen.

# Waypoint 8

*Steps of commitment*

> But as he considered these things, behold, an angel of the Lord appeared to him in a dream, saying, "Joseph, son of David, do not fear to take Mary as your wife, for that which is conceived in her is from the Holy Spirit. She will bear a son, and you shall call his name Jesus, for he will save his people from their sins." All this took place to fulfill what the Lord had spoken by the prophet: "Behold, the virgin shall conceive and bear a son, and they shall call his name Immanuel" (which means, God with us). When Joseph woke from sleep, he did as the angel of the Lord commanded him: he took his wife, but knew her not until she had given birth to a son. And he called his name Jesus. (Matthew 1:20–25)

Reflect

Commitment is a word military folks know well. Joining the military *requires* an obligated time commitment. And for many military personnel, commitment includes not only a timeframe but an ideological ideal accompanied by a strong sense of duty.[19]

Joseph and Mary would have made a good military family. Individually and as a couple they rank high on the commitment scale. Consider the comment by Mary in Luke 1:38 following the angel's announcement that she would carry a child conceived unnaturally: "Behold, I am the servant of the Lord; let it be to me according to your word." In that moment Mary made a commitment to yield to God's will and to trust God with the next step. She rose from that place of divine encounter and set out on a journey of unprecedented trust.

Now consider Joseph, who took a colossal step of commitment in marrying Mary. This was no easy commitment—an angel had to appear to him in a dream for him to say yes! Yet Joseph too made a commitment to yield to God's will and trust God with the next step. He too, rose from a place of divine encounter to set out on a journey of unprecedented trust.

Joseph and Mary started their journey together lacking the answers to some major questions. But isn't that the way it always is when we make vows in marriage? Our commitment to each other says, "I trust you without knowing all the answers."

Sara Horn, an author and military wife, reminds us that commitment must be a starting point to any successful military marriage. "Loving feelings can come and go," she writes, "but commitment creates a bond that is hard to break. When you both wholeheartedly agree, for better or for worse, to be there for the other no matter what, you are that much stronger to withstand the problems that will come."[20]

Military marriage takes a couple on a journey that will test commitment, but each step can give trust the space for unprecedented growth.

### Respond

How has the military tested trust and commitment in your marriage? How are you allowing the military to grow trust and commitment in your marriage?

### Prayer for the journey

Lord, commitment means determination and perseverance in the *no matter what* times in my marriage. Keep my husband and me moving forward in our commitment to one another—especially in times when our commitment is tested. Thank you for this military life and the way you use it to strengthen my marriage. Amen.

# Waypoint 9

*Vulnerable is not a bad word*

> In those days a decree went out from Caesar Augustus
> that all the world should be registered.... And all went
> to be registered, each to his own town. And Joseph also
> went up from Galilee, from the town of Nazareth, to
> Judea, to the city of David, which is called Bethlehem,
> because he was of the house and lineage of David, to
> be registered with Mary, his betrothed, who was with
> child. (Luke 2:1–5)

**Reflect**

Take one pregnant woman, add a PCS order, and you have a
textbook example of the word *vulnerable*. Online military forums
feature questions about the wisdom of making a permanent
change of station while pregnant. Questions come from both
the spouse and the service member concerning everything from
regulations to transfer of medical records.

Karen, a veteran military wife, recalls a PCS move from Texas
to Georgia. She had an energetic toddler and was pregnant with
her second child. Her family was more than ready to leave Texas,
but there was no hurrying the process, Karen recalls. "It took
forever! My husband's out-processing was delayed. We had car
trouble. My sister was coming to help me, and her flight was late.
We did not even make it out of Texas when our car threw a rod.
We had to buy a new vehicle en route. I describe that day as the
day we made it to Waco, but I was wacko!"

Karen can look back now and laugh at the situation. But in
the moment she felt vulnerable. She wanted to trust her husband
during this time, but the circumstances made her question the

wisdom of military service. Working through such a vulnerable situation requires trust.

Mary had to trust Joseph in traveling the ninety miles from Nazareth to Bethlehem.[21] Ninety miles does not seem far—until you consider Mary was pregnant and most likely traveled the unpaved hill trails on a donkey![22] As we saw, an angel visited Mary to tell her she would be the mother of the Son of the Most High. But Luke ends the account by stressing that "the angel departed from her" (Luke 1:26–38). No biblical record mentions an angel traveling with Mary to Bethlehem. The road was dangerous! Wild animals were a constant hazard. Bandits lurked in the shadows; history records that some travelers gave over their wives to protect themselves.[23] Mary had no way to defend herself. She had no way of knowing when the baby would arrive, or where he would be born. She was vulnerable.

It's not a comfortable feeling. Yet in marriage, vulnerability can be a strength. As researcher Brené Brown explains, it can lead to trust: "Trust is a product of vulnerability that grows over time and requires work, attention, and full engagement."[24]

The whole scene begs the question of whether Mary would have gone on the journey if she did not trust Joseph. Her vulnerability validates her trust in this man. Even more, her vulnerability validates her trust in God.

### Respond

In what ways has military life made you vulnerable? How can you use your vulnerability to build trust in your marriage?

### Prayer for the journey

Lord, I repeat: I don't like to be vulnerable! Yet you can use the places where I feel weak and afraid to make me strong in you. Help me to trust you. Give me a willing heart to do the work of building trust in my marriage. Make me fully attentive and engaged toward that purpose. Amen.

# Waypoint 10
## *Ready or not*

> Now when they had departed, behold, an angel of the
> Lord appeared to Joseph in a dream and said, "Rise, take
> the child and his mother, and flee to Egypt, and remain
> there until I tell you, for Herod is about to search for the
> child, to destroy him." (Matthew 2:13)

Reflect

*Ready or not* could be the tagline for military marriage. Army
wife Ruth recalls the Christmas banquet she and her Ranger
husband were attending when her husband received a call from
his unit. He went outside to take the call and did not come back
to the banquet. When she returned home, he was gone. A few
days later, he was parachuting into an armed conflict in Panama.

Ready or not, such a call can come in the middle of the
night, the middle of a dinner, or the middle of a vacation and
usher your husband from your presence without a moment's
notice. Duty calls and he must answer. When the unexpected is
the norm, we often struggle to build trust.

Mary and Joseph had several *ready or not* moments. One is
recorded in Matthew 2:13. Jesus was about two years old, and
King Herod, troubled by the visit of the wise men, was about
to send men to kill all the male babies in Bethlehem up to two
years of age to make sure he eliminated the newborn king-to-be.
On the orders of an angel in a dream, Joseph awakened Mary
in the middle of the night, packed up their belongings, and fled
from Bethlehem to Egypt. If Mary had not trusted Joseph, she
might have told him to go back to sleep and they would talk

about it in the morning. Instead they began a trip that meant riding a donkey or walking for two hundred miles through desert, mountains, and wilderness—*with a two year old.*

I do not have to use much imagination to believe that Mary was less than thrilled with this PCS. Yet there is no indication that she doubted Joseph.[25] She did not have time to plan or prepare for the midnight move. She could not check off her list of things to do because she did not even have time to make a list. Joseph had to take life-or-death action. She trusted that he had her and her baby's interest at heart. At this point, she had to act out of the trust she had nurtured and sustained in her husband because of her trust in God.

The everyday uncertainties that come with military life make trust an essential factor in marriage—and make trusting in God paramount.

### Respond

How would you respond if your husband asked you to do what Joseph asked of Mary? What are some of the *ready or not* moments you have experienced with military life? What part has trust played in those moments?

### Prayer for the journey

Lord, make me ready for whatever you ask of me. Help me trust you and trust my husband as we continue our marriage journey. Amen.

# Waypoint 11

*Isaac and Rebekah—failure to communicate*

Read Genesis 24

And Isaac went out to meditate in the field toward evening. And he lifted up his eyes and saw, and behold, there were camels coming. And Rebekah lifted up her eyes, and when she saw Isaac, she dismounted from the camel and said to the servant, "Who is that man, walking in the field to meet us?" The servant said, "It is my master." So she took her veil and covered herself. And the servant told Isaac all the things that he had done. Then Isaac brought her into the tent of Sarah his mother and took Rebekah, and she became his wife, and he loved her. So Isaac was comforted after his mother's death. (Genesis 24:63–67)

### Reflect

Over the next few waypoints, we will encounter in the marriage of Isaac and Rebekah a case study in the challenge of relational communication. Their marriage began with a noteworthy journey—but it was not a journey the couple made together. In an ancient-world precursor to mail-order brides and online dating, Abraham sent his servant to find a wife for his son Isaac. God had promised to bless Abraham and make his descendants as numerous as the stars in the sky and the sand on the shore (Genesis 15:5; 22:17). The blessing would continue through Isaac and on down the family line. But Abraham was now a very old man and Isaac was not married. Abraham wanted to be sure that Isaac married someone from his own country, so he took matters into his own hands and sent his servant to find Isaac a wife.

The servant spotted a woman named Rebekah at the community well. Her kindness to him—and his weary camels—was impressive (Genesis 24:10–22). She communicated through word and action that she would make a good wife for Isaac, and they met after the servant asked God to lead him to the right girl. He explained the story of his quest to Rebekah and her family and she agreed to return with him (v. 34–58). She showed great courage by her willingness to leave her country, travel to a foreign land, and marry a man she had never met.[26]

Arranged marriage was common in Rebekah and Isaac's culture, but even though the Bible tells us that the couple fell for each other, they did not establish good communication practices before becoming man and wife. Most of us today personally select our own spouses-to-be and arrange our own marriages, but it is still easy to fall into poor communication habits.

Over the next few days, we will look at this marriage that started out strong with God's confirmation, Rebekah's willingness, and Isaac's love. These two soon made choices that led their marriage down a trail of deceit and manipulation.[27] Their later challenges were due in large part to poor communication. We have lessons to learn from their challenges in communication that will help us build stronger marriages.

### Respond

What are some of the communication challenges that can arise in a military marriage? Take time to list the strengths and weaknesses of your marriage in the area of communication. Make this list a focus for your prayer over the next week.

### Prayer for the journey

Lord, I pray my husband and I will listen to one another. Give each of us a heart to hear even if we do not speak with words. Show us the things that disrupt the lines of communication in our marriage. Amen.

# Waypoint 12

*Unfulfilled expectations*

Read

> These are the generations of Isaac, Abraham's son:
> Abraham fathered Isaac, and Isaac was forty years old
> when he took Rebekah ... to be his wife. And Isaac
> prayed to the LORD for his wife, because she was barren.
> And the LORD granted his prayer, and Rebekah his wife
> conceived. (Genesis 25:19–21)

Reflect

Isaac and Rebekah seemed like the perfect couple. Their future looked bright. They started their relationship with love. But something went missing. God had promised the blessing of children through Isaac, and there were none. Do the math after reading on a few verses to Genesis 25:26 and you will discover that Isaac and Rebecca had been married twenty years before Rebekah became pregnant. This was not what either of them expected.[28]

We have a somewhat better understanding of conception now, but in ancient days if there were no children, people would conclude that something was wrong with the woman. Scripture records nothing to indicate whether Rebekah communicated the disappointment of her barrenness with Isaac, nor does it indicate if Isaac offered understanding support. But twenty years is an extremely long time and it is safe to conclude that Rebekah suffered because of her childlessness.[29]

Think of the pressure Rebekah must have felt. When you consider that Isaac knew of God's promise to his father Abraham that a great nation was to come through Isaac, the expectation on Rebekah to produce a son had to be overwhelming. Tension between these two built up over the years, leading to poor communication between them.[30]

Consider your military marriage. What did you expect when you married a military man? Kay expected to see the world, but her husband's first assignment was three hours from her hometown. Annie thought that since her husband did not have to punch a time card anymore, and worked a mile away, he would be available 24/7. Carrie thought she would be able to have her pick of any of the houses on her military installation. Melinda thought filling out a military dream sheet meant her family would have their pick of assignments. Shanna thought she would be the most important priority of her husband—and then duty called.

Unfulfilled expectations may leave us feeling disappointed and resentful. As we replace hopes and dreams with sadness, tension, anger, or conflict, we can become trapped in the breeding ground of poor communication. It may encourage us to realize that Isaac and Rebekah, whose marriage was a part of God's divine plan, struggled with unfulfilled expectations too. We can choose to respond differently than they did, for sharing disappointments honestly with our spouse can actually enhance our understanding of each other and strengthen our relationship.

### Respond

What were some of your preconceived expectations of marriage? What expectations did you have for life as a military wife? How do you manage unfulfilled expectations?

### Prayer for the journey

Lord, protect my marriage from the disappointment of unfulfilled expectations. Help us to identify any issue that keeps us from communicating with honesty. Amen.

# Waypoint 13

*I should have told you*

### Read

> The children struggled together within her, and she said, "If it is thus, why is this happening to me?" So she went to inquire of the LORD. And the LORD said to her, "Two nations are in your womb, and two peoples from within you shall be divided; the one shall be stronger than the other, the older shall serve the younger." When her days to give birth were completed, behold, there were twins in her womb. (Genesis 25:22–24)

### Reflect

Military wives learn to withhold information—for good reason. Consider OPSEC (Operations Security), the process to protect even unclassified information that an adversary can use to harm us. We consistently observe safety measures to minimize risk to our husband and family. A military wife may also purposely withhold details from her husband during a deployment so that he can focus on his mission. But in normal life, withholding information from a spouse is not best practice for a successful marriage.

In Genesis 25:21 we learn that Isaac prayed for Rebekah to conceive. He did not lose hope in the promise of God.[31] God heard Isaac's prayer and Rebekah finally—after twenty years of marriage—became pregnant with twins. The pregnancy was extremely difficult, and her own prayer reveals her feelings: "why is this happening to me?" God's response was a message of insight for the future nation of Israel. The word was not simply to comfort her, it revealed the disturbing destiny of her sons.[32] Her two babies would become two nations—and the older would serve the younger!

She prayed and God answered. Not only did God answer, the passage tells us: *God spoke to her.* Put yourself in that situation. What would you do if "the Lord said" something to you about the future of your children? I would find my husband and relay every word of the message to him—in detail! And I would repeat it to myself several times for emphasis. Rebekah, however, kept the Lord's words to herself. Why would she withhold this significant information from Isaac? Did she feel inferior to Isaac, unable to express herself freely? Did she not want to trouble Isaac with the knowledge that there would be lifelong strife between their children? Did she simply choose to deceive?

We do not know the reason. Scripture simply informs us of the devastating result. Isaac favored the older child Esau and Rebekah favored the younger child Jacob (Genesis 25:27–28). God let Rebekah know Esau was unsuited for the promised blessing, but she did not share that information with Isaac. Her inability or unwillingness to communicate with her husband led to a series of tragedies to the family.[33]

Honesty and openness are fundamental to a strong and healthy marriage. OPSEC within a marriage means not withholding information pertaining to your relationship or family, but sharing despite fear and insecurity.

### Respond

Write your husband a note to communicate your gratitude and love for him. Consider reading the book *The Five Love Languages: Military Edition* with your spouse.[34] The authors propose that we each have an emotional love language, and knowing this about our spouse can help us better navigate communication in marriage.

### Prayer for the journey

Lord, use my words today to bless and encourage my husband. Build our relationship as we learn to communicate better. Help us not make assumptions that lead to misunderstanding. Amen.

# Waypoint 14

*A recipe for disaster*

When Isaac was old and his eyes were dim so that he could not see, he called Esau his older son and said to him, "My son"; and he answered, "Here I am." He said, "Behold, I am old; I do not know the day of my death. Now then, take your weapons, your quiver and your bow, and go out to the field and hunt game for me, and prepare for me delicious food, such as I love, and bring it to me so that I may eat, that my soul may bless you before I die."

Now Rebekah was listening when Isaac spoke to his son Esau. So when Esau went to the field to hunt for game and bring it, Rebekah said to her son Jacob, "I heard your father speak to your brother Esau ... Now therefore, my son, obey my voice as I command you. Go to the flock and bring me two good young goats, so that I may prepare from them delicious food for your father, such as he loves. And you shall bring it to your father to eat, so that he may bless you before he dies." (Genesis 27:1–10).

## Reflect

Bobbi Ann Finley was dubbed the "Military Mistress" after she married 14 different U.S. military service members and stole their money. The state of Alabama sentenced her to three years in prison for theft by deception.[35] She moved from one military installation to another collecting husbands as others collect travel souvenirs. That is serious deception! Obviously, Bobbi Ann failed to share some important details when she said "I do" 14 times.

Isaac and Rebekah also faced deception in their marriage. Rebekah withheld the information that God planned the younger son to inherit the blessing, so Rebekah favored Jacob and Isaac favored Esau. Genesis 27 begins with Isaac preparing to deliver the patriarchal blessing to Esau—and presumably he did not discuss his plan with Rebekah. He had to know it would upset her. They would not agree, so why bother? But Rebekah overheard and devised a plan of her own.

The picture of Rebekah eavesdropping is unflattering, and gives credence to her *next* deceptive actions. As the oldest son, Esau was the rightful heir to his father's blessing—and such a blessing was like a legally binding will today.[36] Blessing Esau would have been legal, yet it was not what God planned. But family dysfunction was not God's plan either.

We can recognize the results: Distrust over time led to deception and manipulation—communication at its worst. Instead of sharing the truth of our fears, hopes, and dreams, we can use our words and actions to manipulate circumstances in our favor. Isaac and Rebekah became master manipulators. Isaac maneuvered so Esau would be the only son present to receive a blessing; Rebekah outmaneuvered Isaac so her favored Jacob would be the one blessed. She left nothing to chance. She even disguised Jacob to make him appear as Esau and prepared food that Esau would have prepared from game killed while hunting (Genesis 27:11–40).[37] Rebekah's meal was a recipe for disaster.

### Respond

Participants in a study on communication in military marriage claimed more intentional communication than did non-military couples.[38] Why could that be true? Have you practiced manipulation or deception in your marriage? What should you change?

### Prayer for the journey

Lord, strengthen military marriages today. I pray for chaplains and counselors to have wisdom and insight as they counsel couples in challenging circumstances. Amen.

# Waypoint 15

*From facts to feelings*

Read Genesis 27:30–45

So she sent and called Jacob her younger son and said to him, "Behold, your brother Esau comforts himself about you by planning to kill you. Now therefore, my son, obey my voice. Arise, flee to Laban my brother in Haran and stay with him a while, until your brother's fury turns away—until your brother's anger turns away from you, and he forgets what you have done to him. Then I will send and bring you from there. Why should I be bereft of you both in one day?" (Genesis 27:42b–45)

## Reflect

Alienation from and between their children was the result of the deceptive practices of Isaac and Rebekah. Who was to blame for their communication fiasco? Looking at the story as a whole, we can conclude that Isaac failed to share his goals with his wife while Rebekah was not forthright with her husband.

When it came to their physical interaction, however, the Bible indicates they communicated very well. Midway in their marriage, Isaac and Rebekah moved for a time to Gerar where we get a glimpse of the physical passion they shared (Genesis 26:8). You may have heard the joke, "What's the second thing your military husband takes off when he comes in from field duty? His rucksack." Your husband might be quick to communicate physically, but it may take more time to share his feelings.

The goal for healthy marriage communication is to complete the journey from facts to feelings. The most basic level of communication is sharing facts and ideas. Think *small talk*. This is not deep—on the order of "How was your day?"—

but such communication connects you to one another as you inform each other about life outside of your relationship.

Sharing facts can only take you so far; you must be willing to share thoughts and ideas. This level of communication becomes more risky and could lead to disagreement and judgment. Trust grows as a couple is willing to hear opinions, discuss differences, and remain open to hearing another view.[39]

The most effective communication is to be able to share feelings and needs. Communication on this level opens the door to understanding. Marriage experts Gary and Barbara Rosberg compare this to exploring a cave "with a vast labyrinth of underground caverns someone could spend a lifetime exploring … every step, every turn in the labyrinth, every new day of exploration yields surprises and challenges too good to miss."[40] The journey to deep, heartfelt communication will not be easy, but the discoveries will be worth the effort.

### Respond

Consider these sure communication killers. Check any you have used with your husband in the last month: ☐ overgeneralizations (always, never); ☐ derogatory names; ☐ ridicule and sarcasm; ☐ offensive comments; ☐ the silent treatment.

Relationship specialist John Gottman instructs couples to work toward a ratio of five positive interactions to every one negative. Positive interactions include such relationship builders as a smile, a touch, changing the course of negative conversation, and positive, affectionate, encouraging comments.[41] Consider the ratio of communication killers to relationship builders in your marriage. How does your marriage math add up?

### Prayer for the journey

Lord, help my marriage to be built on wisdom and established through understanding (Proverbs 24:3). Amen.

# Waypoint 16

*Jacob and Rachel—you marry a family*

> Then Jacob went on his journey and came to the land of the people of the east. (Genesis 29:1)

> Now as soon as Jacob saw Rachel the daughter of Laban his mother's brother, and the sheep of Laban his mother's brother, Jacob came near and rolled the stone from the well>s mouth and watered the flock of Laban his mother's brother. Then Jacob kissed Rachel and wept aloud. And Jacob told Rachel that he was her father's kinsman, and that he was Rebekah's son, and she ran and told her father. As soon as Laban heard the news about Jacob, his sister's son, he ran to meet him and embraced him and kissed him and brought him to his house. (Genesis 29:10–13a)

Reflect

As we saw, with the help of his mother, Jacob tricked his father Isaac out of the blessing that rightfully belonged to his older brother Esau. In fear of retribution from Esau and at his mother's suggestion, Jacob fled to the land of his uncle Laban. There he encountered the beautiful Rachel and fell hopelessly in love with her. The story has the feel of a Hollywood movie, complete with a show of strength from the leading man, long arduous glances, a kiss, and even tears. It is quite a moving story—until Rachel's dad inserts himself.

They say you do not just marry a person, you marry a family. The truth is, you marry into a family and you have to deal with the customs, behaviors, and attitudes embedded in that family. You have to take the family's claims on your spouse into consideration. In Jacob's case, his greedy future father-in-law's claim on Rachel frustrated Jacob's immediate marriage plans. Laban agreed to allow Jacob to marry Rachel, but he did not keep his word. Instead he tricked Jacob into first marrying his daughter Leah. Though Laban then allowed Jacob to marry Rachel, he required an additional seven years of work. Do not miss the detail that Laban was Jacob's uncle. His sharp dealings give an indication of his character; he shows a pattern more like an oppressive lord over a contracted servant rather than a supportive uncle helping a relative. Yes, Jacob ran headlong into in-law problems from the moment he met Rachel.

On the one hand, you might say that with Laban Jacob met his match and got some of his just desserts for his selfish actions with his own family. On the other hand, you can see through Jacob's willingness to work hard and fulfill a contract that God used this situation to refine his character.[42]

Western culture does not practice attaching a dollar amount to a spouse anymore, but families still exert a sense of "ownership" that couples must take into consideration. No couple is immune from challenges that arise from their family-of-origin experiences. Each couple must learn to celebrate the differences and turn them into strengths as you value what each brings into a marriage.[43]

### Respond

What challenges have you experienced with in-laws because of military life? What joys have you experienced with in-laws because of military life?

### Prayer for the journey

Lord, thank you for my in-laws. If not for them, I would not know my husband. I pray your blessings upon them. Help us to have a good and positive relationship of mutual support. Amen.

# Waypoint 17

*Obey vs. honor*

Read

So Jacob served seven years for Rachel, and they seemed to him but a few days because of the love he had for her. (Genesis 29:20)

Then Jacob said to Laban, "Give me my wife that I may go in to her, for my time is completed." So Laban gathered together all the people of the place and made a feast. But in the evening he took his daughter Leah and brought her to Jacob, and he went in to her.... And in the morning, behold, it was Leah! And Jacob said to Laban, "What is this you have done to me? Did I not serve with you for Rachel? Why then have you deceived me?" (Genesis 29:21–25)

Reflect

If the requirement of working seven years to marry Rachel does not give Laban a place on the list for most awful father-in-law ever, his next move seals the deal. The seven years Jacob worked for Rachel's hand in marriage seemed to him just a few days because of his love for her. The day of the wedding arrived, but instead of joy in uniting with his beloved Rachel, Jacob was devastated when he discovered Laban had tricked him into marrying her older sister Leah. Laban gave his permission for Jacob to marry Rachel after a week, but only following another agreement to work for him another seven years! Even with polygamy an accepted practice in the ancient Near East, this was unacceptable.

In-law jokes abound, but there is no humor in a poor relationship with your in-laws. Such a relationship can be an ongoing source of conflict. In Jacob's case the conflict with his oppressive father-in-law lasted twenty years.[44] Laban demonstrated his dependence on Jacob for his own prosperity— he manipulated him to get rich.[45] Another term for this type of dependence is *enmeshment.*

In an enmeshed family system, parents are dependent on their children to make them feel fulfilled. Laban's conniving and controlling behavior is a clear symptom of enmeshment. He involved Jacob, Rachel, and Leah in a difficult situation that was almost impossible to escape.

The expectations placed on all members of a family following a marriage can be unrealistic and overwhelming. Kay recalls feeling threatened and intimidated by her strong-willed mother-in-law. Her husband offered wise advice early in their marriage: "Listen to my mother, and then do what you think *you* should do." Scripture tells us that we are to obey our parents, but *obey* transitions to *honor* when a couple marries.

In their book *Loving Your Relatives,* David and Claudia Arp suggest ways to navigate the often complicated in-law relationship:

- Be proactive and look for ways to connect.
- Don't compete with other family members.
- Refocus your perspective by looking for the positive.
- Accept reality.[46]

### Respond

What kind of relationship do you have with your in-laws? Even if you have a good relationship, there is always room for improvement. What is one thing you can do today to connect positively with your in-laws?

### Prayer for the journey

Lord, help my husband and me to find creative ways to connect with our parents. Help us to honor our parents even when we do not agree with them. Amen.

# Waypoint 18
## *The Brady Bunch does not live here*

> When Rachel saw that she bore Jacob no children, she
> envied her sister. She said to Jacob, "Give me children,
> or I shall die!" Jacob's anger was kindled against Rachel,
> and he said, "Am I in the place of God who has withheld
> from you the fruit of the womb?" (Genesis 30:1–2)

Reflect

In-law problems were not the only problems Jacob encountered
in marriage. Now he had not only one wife, but two—two
sisters who brought their own baggage into the complicated
relationship. No, this is not an episode of *Sister-Wives,* but the
ancient day equivalent of a blended family.

The Pew Research Center reports that there are more
blended families today than in any other time in history. Nearly
half of young people ages 18 to 29 have a stepsibling.[47] Cru
Military believes the number of blended families in the military
far exceeds the ratio in the general population.[48] Blending a
family is a challenge, and military life adds additional factors to
that challenge. Cru's Ron Deal says that the average stepfamily
needs five to seven years to develop a family identity. Military
families may see this timeframe extended due to the absence of
a parent through deployment, training, or operations tempo.
Deal suggests a new blended military family "step down" their
expectations and be patient as they adjust to the new situation.[49]

The configuration of a blended family varies as do the challenges. The old "Brady Bunch" scenario is not the norm for such
families. Before the new family settles in together the common

state of affairs includes power struggles, boundary testing, and guilt. In the case of Jacob, Rachel, and Leah, the situation brought jealousy and drama. Rachel and Leah worked against each other in their effort to be the favored wife. Their competition for social standing through bearing children brought disgrace to Jacob and planted seeds of tribalism that would be evident through their children.[50]

Yet, through all the deception, drama, competition, jealousy, and blame, God worked his plan. Theologian Walter Brueggemann describes the scene: "... two competitive sisters, a husband caught between them, and an exploitive father-in-law are not the most likely data for narratives of faith."[51] Indeed. Yet God did use these fallen and fallible people. God blessed this blended family with twelve sons through whom God fulfilled his promise to Abraham to establish a great nation from his heirs.

### Respond

You may be a member of a blended family. If so, what have been your unique challenges to adjust to military life? Consider a blended military family you know. How can you bless them today?

### Prayer for the journey

Lord, I pray your blessings on the family I just identified, and all blended military families. You know the unique challenges they face. Help them as they navigate their way to becoming a united and strong family unit. Amen.

# Waypoint 19
*United we stand*

Read

So Jacob sent and called Rachel and Leah into the field where his flock was and said to them, "I see that your father does not regard me with favor as he did before. But the God of my father has been with me. You know that I have served your father with all my strength, yet your father has cheated me and changed my wages ten times. But God did not permit him to harm me." (Genesis 31:4–7)

Then Rachel and Leah answered and said to him, "Is there any portion or inheritance left to us in our father's house? Are we not regarded by him as foreigners? For he has sold us, and he has indeed devoured our money. All the wealth that God has taken away from our father belongs to us and to our children. Now then, whatever God has said to you, do." (Genesis 31:14–16)

### Reflect

Rachel and Leah took initiative to change their situation. Jacob called a family meeting and—perhaps surprisingly—these three had a calm discussion about their future. They created a united front against Laban and his injustice. Together they conversed as partners, made a decision, and stood in solidarity concerning their next move.[52] They united in purpose, voice, and action as they decided to leave Laban and move to Canaan.[53]

Family challenges have the potential to create closeness or bring division. Early in his marriage, Steven felt compelled to connect with his parents about the challenging issues he faced as a husband. His parents were good and godly people but did not at first recognize the danger in Steven's dependence upon them. They convinced themselves that their discussions were "wise counsel." When Steven's wife realized these discussions were going on without her, she felt justifiably threatened.

Steven's mom recalls the night she received a call from her son. "He told us he felt convicted for coming to us and in essence complaining about his wife. He said he needed to practice working things out with his wife instead of griping to us about her. I felt sad and happy at the same time. Sad that our connection with him would change, but happy and proud that the change would be a healthy move toward my son cherishing his wife and becoming more united as a couple."

Steven's mom reports that her son and his wife continue to have challenges, but now they work together to resolve their issues and have become closer as a result. No family is immune to challenges, but we can look at every challenge as an opportunity to grow closer, and every difficulty as an opportunity to stand united.

### Respond

How united is the front in your home? Is there something you need to do in order to stand united?

### Prayer for the journey

Lord, I pray you would allow my husband and me to stand united in purpose, voice, and action. May we be at peace as we share decision making. Help us to work together, lean on each other, and seek your will when we face challenges and difficulties. Amen.

# Waypoint 20
*Setting boundaries*

"Come now, let us make a covenant, you and I. And let it be a witness between you and me." So Jacob took a stone and set it up as a pillar. And Jacob said to his kinsmen, "Gather stones." And they took stones and made a heap, and they ate there by the heap. Laban called it Jegar-sahadutha, but Jacob called it Galeed. Laban said, "This heap is a witness between you and me today." Therefore he named it Galeed, and Mizpah, for he said, "The LORD watch between you and me, when we are out of one another's sight. (Genesis 31:44–49)

Early in the morning Laban arose and kissed his grandchildren and his daughters and blessed them. Then Laban departed and returned home (Genesis 31:55).

Reflect

Jacob and his wives departed secretly for Canaan (Genesis 31:17–21). When Laban discovered they were gone, he was furious. He determined to find his daughters and that scoundrel of a son-in-law, and bring them back to his home. The difference between the journey of Laban and the journey of Jacob is that God called Jacob on this journey (31:3, 11–13). In fact, God warned Laban in a dream not to harm Jacob (31:24, 29). God's protection was upon Jacob as he traveled.

The distrust this family felt toward one another was strong, but the purposes of God were stronger. God had plans for Jacob and his family. A confrontation with Laban was overdue, and some family boundaries needed to be set. The men aired over twenty years of grievances and made stipulations for future interaction.[54] They gathered a pile of stones as a public witness to the vow of peace they were making. They called on God to witness: "The Lord watch between you and me, when we are out of one another's sight" (Genesis 31:49b).[55] And the two swore they would not pass the pile of stones with the intent to harm each other (31:51–52).

The boundaries set by Jacob and Laban were literal stones that marked the boundaries to the land of Laban and the land of Jacob.[56] Setting boundaries meant the end of trouble from Jacob's difficult father-in-law. The cycle of his interference was broken.

Setting boundaries is an important concept in any family. Healthy boundaries allow for peaceful coexistence. Within extended families, clarify expectations on such things as where to spend the holidays, how to discipline your children, and how often to interact or visit. Boundaries provide protective parameters in a relationship. Jacob's family could not control Laban, but they could put some distance between them and set boundaries to protect their relationship from further damage.

### Respond

Military families often find it challenging to navigate deployments, especially overseas assignments. How have you managed such situations—while preparing, during the assignment, and on your return? What boundaries have you set, or do you see the need to set, with your extended family?

### Prayer for the journey

Lord, help me and my husband to set wise boundaries in all of our relationships. Amen.

# Waypoint 21

*Proverbs 31—Stewardship in marriage*

An excellent wife who can find? She is far more precious than jewels. (Proverbs 31:10)

Reflect

My friend Linda declares that the woman described in Proverbs 31 has to be a military wife! The woman is the definition of resourceful—and she can be intimidating. You have met this military wife, haven't you? She is in great physical shape and runs in every charity race. She volunteers for countless community activities while operating her own home-based business. She opens her home for gatherings after spending the day taking cookies to troops in military billets. She is at every military function, always dressed in red, white, and blue. Perhaps I exaggerate.

The book of Proverbs is a book of wisdom. Put wisdom into practice and Proverbs 31:10–31 will be the result.[57] The woman of Proverbs 31 does not describe a particular woman, but an ideal. She is an example to instruct both women and men on the path of wisdom.[58] The Hebrew language describes her as a *woman of valor.* She is not portrayed as passive or self-indulgent, but as wise and conscientious. She is a woman of substance and courage. The term translated as *excellent wife* is from the Hebrew word *hayil.* Referring to physical strength and bravery, *hayil* is commonly associated with those who serve with courage and loyalty—including those serving in the military.[59]

One message of Proverbs 31:10 is that people are worth more than money or things. We must keep the perspective that the worth of a person and the worth of a relationship are far greater than mere money in the bank. When you read the description of this woman, you see her value lies in her personal qualities of diligence and intelligence, not in the material wealth she gained.

Among the top stressors of marriage is the availability and stewardship of a couple's financial resources. Stresses related to finances can affect every other area of married life. But you do not have to be financially wealthy to be financially healthy. You only need a united view of the way you will steward your resources.

### Respond

On a scale of 1 to 10 with "1" being unhealthy and "10" being very healthy, where would you rate your financial health? What do you and your husband need to do to get closer to 10?

### Prayer for the journey

Lord, thank you for all you have provided my family. Help us to be wise stewards of the provisions with which you have blessed us. Amen.

# Waypoint 22

*He trusts her completely*

Read

> The heart of her husband trusts in her, and he will have
> no lack of gain. She does him good, and not harm, all
> the days of her life. (Proverbs 31:11–12)

Reflect

Michele is a young woman I met during a retreat for deployed spouses. I watched her through the week we were together. She was fully present for her two daughters even though frequent issues arose from her home-based business. She calmly dealt with the issues, working hard to tie up loose ends so she could take part in the retreat sessions and enjoy free time with her girls. I will be the first to shout from the rooftops that military wives are among the most resourceful women on the planet, and in Michele I met the leader of the pack. I've continued to watch Michele via social media as she welcomed her husband home following deployment and continues to blossom in her career. Her industrious ways remind me of the woman in Proverbs 31:11–12.

I dare say Michele's husband celebrates her value to him not because of the money she makes from her successful business, but in the complete trust he has in her. Her husband is a warrior in the U.S. military, but Michele is a warrior of a different kind. The word used in this passage for "gain" is another military term. The literal meaning in Hebrew is *spoils of war*. The woman in Proverbs 31 is like a warrior who brings home loot from her victories.[60] She makes sure her family has everything they need to survive.

This woman is not fighting a losing battle with a credit card balance or uncontrolled spending. No, she fights tenaciously and effectively to bring in resources. Her husband has confidence that her battles in this arena are for the good of their family.

Trust, of course, is a two-way street. I remind you: this passage may be written about a woman, but the wisdom taught is for all. Finances will be an issue in marriage if there is a low level of trust between both husband and wife.

### Respond

What kind of battle are you and your husband fighting in the area of finances? Can you both say you trust each other where money is concerned?

### Prayer for the journey

Lord, sometimes I do not agree with how my husband spends money, and sometimes he does not agree with how I spend money. Help us to respect and trust each other. Guide us as we become better managers of the resources you have placed in our hands. Amen.

# Waypoint 23

*She works willingly*

> She seeks wool and flax, and works with willing hands.
> She is like the ships of the merchant; she brings her
> food from afar. (Proverbs 31:13–14)

## Reflect

As I look up from my computer, my eyes fall upon a vignette of blue and white objects. Each one tells a story from my military journey. I see the vase I purchased in East Berlin before the fall of the Berlin Wall, the plates with images of famous places where we lived in Wiesbaden, Germany, the mug from Japan, the platter from Korea, the ginger jar from Hong Kong, and the lapis box my husband sent from Afghanistan.

I enjoyed collecting my blue and white treasures from around the world, but a house of international mementos is not what is communicated in Proverbs 31:13–14. I am afraid that I sometimes do not have "willing hands" or a joyful spirit for trips closer to home to purchase household supplies. I know others enjoy going to the grocery store. I am not that girl.

The good thing for me is that I do not have to be that girl. Between my husband and me, one of us will go to the grocery store. (Fortunately, he likes to make that trip—it is one of the many reasons I love him!) The point is not whether or not I like to go to the grocery store; the point is whether I am a person who is willing to meet the needs of my family. The heart and goal of the entire chapter is found in these two verses. The focus of this woman of wisdom is not to collect personal treasures but to do whatever her willing hands need to do to care for her family.

### Respond

What does it mean to you to "work with willing hands"? In what ways do you and your husband "work with willing hands" to provide for the needs of your family?

### Prayer for the journey

Lord, help me to always remember that people are more important than things. Help my family know they are a priority and a blessing in my life. Amen.

# Waypoint 24

*She invests wisely*

> She considers a field and buys it; with the fruit
> of her hands she plants a vineyard. She dresses
> herself with strength and makes her arms strong.
> She perceives that her merchandise is profitable. Her
> lamp does not go out at night. (Proverbs 31:16–18)

I know many military wives who travel to an upcoming duty
station to rent or purchase a home *sans* husband. Words like
equity, escrow, amortization, earnest money, HUD, VHA, and
closing costs do not intimidate these warrior sisters. They are
like the woman who buys a field in Proverbs 31.

I am not suggesting you aspire to make such a big decision
as purchasing a house on your own. What I will suggest is that
you follow the example described in Proverbs 31:16. Whether
alone or together, you need to follow two principles we see
described in this verse.

First, give proper consideration before making a major
purchase. Decide if this is the best thing for you to do at this
time. In the case of a home, weigh the competing factors of
buying, renting, or living on a military installation. During my
husband's first military assignment, we had assumed that buying
a home was the best thing to do. We met with a realtor and even
put earnest money down for a house. We knew nothing about
military life and did not realize that our quality of life would be
higher if we lived on that particular military installation. When
we realized this, we ended up having to give up our earnest

money to live in military quarters, but we have never regretted that decision. We have not always lived on military installations, but at that time it was the best choice.

We see the second principle in the way the wise woman in Proverbs 31:16 planted a vineyard. She had a long-term goal and did not expect immediate gratification. You do not get fruit right after planting. It will often be years before you can profit from mature crops. The principle is to look ahead at how major financial decisions will affect your future.

Your family's financial situation needs to strengthen you as a family unit. Your confidence in each other will grow with each good decision. You can better enjoy what you have today when you view it as an investment in your future. Soon you can be in a position to do the things you want, have the things you need, and live in generosity because you do not live paycheck to paycheck.

### Respond

What is your family plan for major purchases? What kind of financial plan do you have for the future?

### Prayer for the journey

Lord, you are my provider. My husband and I need your help to have the discipline to develop a financial plan for the future. Strengthen our will to be debt-free and know the joy of financial freedom. Amen.

# Waypoint 25

*She gives generously*

> She opens her hand to the poor and reaches out her
> hands to the needy. (Proverbs 31:20)

Did you know that the more generous married spouses are to each other, the happier they are? It is true. The National Marriage Project has confirmed that having an attitude of generosity and forgiveness helps to protect a marriage.[61] Research also confirms that generosity within a marriage begets generosity outside of marriage. Couples who are generous to one another will in turn be generous to others.[62]

You can see this principle at work in the life of the Proverbs 31 family. A generous spirit was at work in this home. The wife was diligent and worked hard to provide for her family and prepare for her future, but she was not blind to those in need around her. She used her hands to work hard, but those same hands reached out to the poor and needy. She worked so she could give.[63]

Generosity takes many forms. The word *poor* in Proverbs 31:20 can apply both to the financial or emotional state of a person. The generous person extends a hand to give what they can out of their resources of time, talent, or treasure. A married couple needs to agree upon the amount of time, talent, or treasure they will share with others.

The ability to share some of your resources with others can only come when you are able to manage those resources. No indication is given that the Proverbs 31 woman ignored her family or other obligations. In addition to meeting their needs, she found ways to help those who needed her help. The generosity this family shared with others was an overflow of the generosity they shared with one another.

## Respond

Have you seen the benefits of generosity inside and outside of marriage? What principles of giving do you find in these Scriptures?

- Proverbs 11:25
- Proverbs 19:17
- Hebrews 13:16
- 2 Corinthians 9:7

## Prayer for the journey

Lord, I pray that my husband and I would be generous. Give us both the desire to budget our money and our schedules so we can give to meet the needs of others. Open our hearts to give out of the abundance of what you have given us in talent, time, and treasure. Amen.

# Waypoint 26

*Aquila and Pricilla—the roles we play*

### Read

After this Paul left Athens and went to Corinth. And he found a Jew named Aquila, a native of Pontus, recently come from Italy with his wife Priscilla, because Claudius had commanded all the Jews to leave Rome. And he went to see them, and because he was of the same trade he stayed with them and worked, for they were tentmakers by trade. (Acts 18:1–3)

### Reflect

We come into marriage with certain ideas of what a wife does in a marriage and what a husband does. What models of marriage have you observed? A traditional model has the wife taking care of the home and the husband taking care of financial support. A common model in the military is the dual-military couple where both husband and wife have an equal level of responsibility at work and share responsibilities at home. We can think of a variety of other models.

The New Testament introduces us to a couple who modeled marriage differently from the culture around them. Aquila and Priscilla were a married couple who owned and operated a tentmaking business. The apostle Paul met them on a ministry journey to Corinth. He was also a tentmaker and this couple became significant to him and to the early church. All six New Testament references to Aquila and Priscilla mention them together. They model marriage partnership at its best.

There is no perfect marriage model. No matter which you follow, you and your husband need to agree on the direction for your marriage. Every marriage requires you both to work together to bring your unique gifts, talents, abilities, and strengths into the union. Operating in your respective strengths will enhance your life as a couple.

The challenge for the military marriage is maintaining flexibility regarding roles. During times of deployment and extended duty, more responsibility falls on the spouse who remains home. But this challenge can serve to further strengthen a couple as they work together to remain close and keep their partnership active.

### Respond

You do not have to work side by side with your spouse like Aquila and Priscilla to have a good marriage. In what ways do you and your spouse demonstrate partnership and teamwork? What is one thing you can do to improve your partnership and teamwork?

### Prayer for the journey

Lord, help my husband and me to function as a team. Show us how to serve one another and teach us how to operate in our respective strengths. Help us work together to strengthen our marriage. Amen.

# Waypoint 27

## *A woman's work?*

> After this, Paul stayed many days longer and then took
> leave of the brothers and set sail for Syria, and with him
> Priscilla and Aquila. (Acts 18:18)

### Reflect

What expectations did you have about the roles of husband
and wife when you entered your marriage? Was one to care for
everything inside the house and another to care for everything
outside? Perhaps you entered marriage expecting a fifty-fifty
deal where you and your husband would share responsibilities
both at home and monetarily through your own vocations.
Our expectations vary according to our family of origin, beliefs,
cultural influences, and other personal experiences.

Consider one couple that walked into the chaplain's office.
The husband asked the chaplain to "fix" his wife. What was the
problem? She could not iron his uniforms in a way that met his
specifications. The scenario seems humorous, but there was
nothing funny about the animosity this couple felt toward each
other because her ironing fell short of his standards!

Another couple went through what they ended up calling
the "Underwear Saga." The first night home after their honey-
moon, the husband threw his underwear on the floor. He continued to do this, and after a few days a pile of underwear gathered. They made their way to the chaplain's office practically
ready for a divorce. Angry because his wife would not pick up
his underwear, he said she was lazy. Angry because her husband
threw his underwear on the floor, she said he was a slob. The
chaplain asked him if he would be willing to throw his under-

wear in a hamper. He asked her if she would be willing to throw the dirty clothes in the washing machine. They agreed to the plan and their marriage got a fresh start—and clean clothes!

They sound ridiculous, but these are true stories! Unspoken assumptions about roles can mark a turn toward marriage disaster. You may expect he will take out the garbage and he may expect you will pick up his underwear—or iron his uniform.

As mentioned, Priscilla and Aquila were a unique couple for their time. When we meet them in Acts, they already seem to have resolved the role issues couples often face. But I imagine Priscilla and Aquila never expected to fill the roles of "missionary team members" and sail to a foreign land alongside a preacher named Paul to help establish a church. This task must have been accompanied by some personal doubts and struggles. But they navigated the expectations of their new roles through mutual respect and shared purpose. With patience, communication, and God's help you and your husband can do the same.

### Respond

Gary Chapman suggests doing an exercise with your husband to clarify role expectations. Make a list of all the things your parents did around your house. What did your father do? What did your mother do? Share your lists and discuss why you think your parents fulfilled those roles in their marriages. Discuss how you would like roles and responsibilities to work in your marriage. Decide your next steps together and be willing to compromise on some expectations in order to move forward with a strong and unified marriage.[64]

### Prayer for the journey

Lord, help my husband and me to mutually support one another. Remind us of our shared purpose as a couple. Give us patience and clear communication to navigate the expectations we have of one another. May our expectations be realistic and protect us from disappointment that would damage our marriage. Amen.

# Waypoint 28

*Marriage mentors*

Now a Jew named Apollos, a native of Alexandria, came to Ephesus. He was an eloquent man, competent in the Scriptures. He had been instructed in the way of the Lord. And being fervent in spirit, he spoke and taught accurately the things concerning Jesus, though he knew only the baptism of John. He began to speak boldly in the synagogue, but when Priscilla and Aquila heard him, they took him aside and explained to him the way of God more accurately. (Acts 18:24–26)

Reflect

*Happily ever after* is not a natural outcome of a wedding. This may burst someone's fantasy marriage bubble, but there is no such thing as a perfect couple—nor a perfect marriage. You can, however, have a good and healthy marriage. The goal is not perfection but a healthy and growing relationship. Often you need other people to help you stay on the road to healthy. In my own marriage, I think of the example of Sandra and Al, who mentored us in serving God in the military. I think of Pat and Sue who mentored us in the art of hospitality—and taught me how to make gravy. Bruce and Karen have mentored us in the area of generosity and service to family and community. None of these couples sat down and taught us a specific *how to* lesson. They mentored us through moments spent in their presence and through our observation of their lives.

Mentoring is a principle seen in the lives of Aquila and Priscilla. Paul mentored them and they in turn mentored

Apollos. Even though he was a good speaker and knew the Old Testament Scriptures and the teaching of John the Baptist, Apollos did not know the full story about Jesus. Aquila and Priscilla listened to him teach and perceived his need for the rest of the gospel story. They took him aside privately and filled in the gaps—that Jesus was the Messiah, that he had been crucified and resurrected, that he had ascended to heaven, that the Holy Spirit had come, and much more.[65]

Together, Priscilla and Aquila invested their lives in building relationships. Their hospitality and mentoring had a powerful influence on the church in Corinth and beyond. Just like the couples who had an impact on my husband and me, Priscilla and Aquila were willing to take the time to help others become better.

Look around for couples you admire, people who are strong in their faith and have qualities you would like to develop in your own marriage. Invite them for coffee or a meal and ask their input on issues that concern you. You do not—and should not—have to make this journey alone. God has placed people and resources to help you grow in your faith and in your relationships. You and your husband also have stories, skills, and lessons learned that you can share with others.

### Respond

Who might you consider as marriage mentors? What questions would you want to ask a marriage mentor?

### Prayer for the journey

Lord, give my husband and me teachable spirits. Open our eyes to people who will encourage us and help our relationship grow stronger. Help us be willing to share what we have learned with others also. Amen.

# Waypoint 29

*Who's on first?*

> Greet Prisca and Aquila, my fellow workers in Christ
> Jesus, who risked their necks for my life, to whom not
> only I give thanks but all the churches of the Gentiles
> give thanks as well. (Romans 16:3–4)

The other night my husband and I watched a snippet of the
famous Abbott and Costello comedy routine, "Who's on
First?" The attempt to explain the lineup of a baseball team and
the confusion that follows is both hilarious and frustrating. It
reminded me of the confusion and frustration that can come in
marriage as we navigate and negotiate "who's on first?"

Have you noticed as you read the Scripture references for
Priscilla (or Prisca)[66] and Aquila that sometimes an author
lists Priscilla first, and other times Aquila is first? A woman's
name preceding a man was unusual for New Testament times.
Scholars have suggested several reasons for this unconventional
listing. Perhaps Priscilla's social standing or family wealth was
greater than that of her husband. Perhaps she became a Christian
before her husband. Perhaps she was the more intellectual of
the two, or the more energetic in ministry and service.[67] The
explanations are speculative, but scholars agree the alternate
listings are not an accident. Whatever the reason, the alternating
order indicates their teamwork.[68] Based on the way this couple
operated, we can surmise that sometimes Priscilla took the lead
and sometimes Aquila took the lead in their work and ministry.

It is common to hear about military wives lamenting their lack of independence, status, and identity. Priscilla was not a military wife, but her society expected her to find status and identity through her husband. Yet the Bible references her first in four of the six listings of their names. How significant! I venture to guess she did not lobby for first listing. She and her husband worked as a team. She did not allow cultural expectations to keep her from fulfilling her call as a wife, career woman, and leader in the church. And Aquila was clearly on board with that line of thinking.

Sisters, do not listen to naysayers who downplay your contribution because you are a military wife. Priscilla did not let any expectations or criticism stop her from fulfilling her God-ordained roles. She worked hard running a business with her husband. She actively labored to establish the early church. She taught and mentored others in their faith. She and her husband launched a church in their home. Along with her husband, she risked her life to protect the apostle Paul when enemies threatened his life. This woman did not let being a woman stop her from living her life fully. It did not matter who was on first; it mattered that she and Aquila knew they were on the same team.

### Respond

What roles are you fulfilling at this time in your life (wife, mother, daughter, employee, volunteer, teacher, other)? Are any of your roles taking away from partnership and teamwork with your husband? If so, what do you need to do to realign your roles to strengthen your marriage?

### Prayer for the journey

Lord, help me to fulfill the roles you have for me as a woman. Help me to understand my value to you and to my husband. Help me do my part to make my marriage a testimony of your grace. Amen.

# Waypoint 30

## 'Their' house

> The churches of Asia send you greetings. Aquila and Prisca, together with the church in their house, send you hearty greetings in the Lord. (1 Corinthians 16:19)

Reflect

We do not know many details about Aquila and Priscilla's marriage. The details we learn from Scripture allow us to piece together a picture of a committed couple. Acts 18:1–3 tells us they fled from Rome to a foreign country after the emperor forced all the Jews to leave. Later, they traveled by ship to Ephesus where they helped Paul evangelize. They seem to have eventually returned to Rome and continued building the early church.

Like military families who move from place to place, Aquila and Priscilla moved many times, committed to fulfill God's purpose for them in each new place. They worked together to serve Christ wherever their journey took them. Their moves most likely were to enhance their service to God than to enhance their tentmaking business. When you see the names of this couple, you read only positive remarks. They saw themselves as a team, and others did as well.

1 Corinthians 16:19 refers to the church in "their" house. This reference does not impress the modern reader, but first-century society, with its male-dominated rights, leadership, and ownership, would have considered this a radical reference.[69] Paul and the early church fully accepted this couple and the way they operated as a team. Paul wrote of his gratitude for Aquila

and Priscilla—and not only *his* gratitude, but the gratitude of all the churches.

Priscilla and Aquila, both individually and together made a difference in their sphere of influence. They established marriage roles that worked for them, were pleasing to God, and helpful for others. If you want your own experiences "until death do us part" to be both long and fulfilling, then strive to have mutually understood and agreed-upon roles. As your life journey progresses, changing circumstances may require new roles, but defining expectations and allowing for flexibility will keep you moving forward together.

## Respond

How can you and your husband serve others together? How could you use your home in service to God?

## Prayer for the journey

Lord, show my husband and me ways we can serve others in our community. Give us something we can do together as an act of service. Give us hearts that beat in unison in our desire to share you.

# Journey 2

*Devoted to My Children*

# Introduction

Holding a newborn baby always reminds me of how dependent a child is on others. Devoted parents lovingly endure sleepless nights, dutiful days, and altered lifestyles to nurture and care for their offspring. Parents celebrate when little ones learn to feed themselves, put on their clothes, and play with other children, and, yes, we grieve a little when they head off to navigate life on their own.

Even with the help of a community—and the military community can be a good one—to rear children, parents have a devotion to the wellbeing of their children that normally we cannot relinquish to others. Every stage of a child's life demands loving guidance and oversight from devoted parents. While the physical needs of children are more visible and often easier to meet, the mental and spiritual needs are more important and can be more complex. Devoted parents demonstrate love to their children by giving attention to all their needs.

A healthy child in all respects is the goal of devoted parents. However, the spiritual needs that have an eternal dimension are most important. Just as parents brought their children to Jesus for him to bless them, devoted parents still bring their children to the Lord. From meaningful rituals that present a young child to the Lord, through early years of Christian education, to a mature life as a Christ-follower, devoted parents play a significant role in the spiritual growth of their children. The waypoints along this thirty-day Journey will provide you with biblical guidance on how to best express parental devotion. Before you start each day, pray this prayer from Psalm 119:18: Lord, "Open my eyes, that I may behold wondrous things out of your law."

See you on the road!

# Waypoint 1

## *At home in an ark*

### Read

The LORD saw that the wickedness of man was great in the earth, and that every intention of the thoughts of his heart was only evil continually. And the LORD regretted that he had made man on the earth, and it grieved him to his heart. So the LORD said, "I will blot out man whom I have created from the face of the land, man and animals and creeping things and birds of the heavens, for I am sorry that I have made them." But Noah found favor in the eyes of the LORD.

These are the generations of Noah. Noah was a righteous man, blameless in his generation. Noah walked with God. And Noah had three sons, Shem, Ham, and Japheth. (Genesis 6:5–10)

### Reflect

Over the years, I have collected several Noah's Ark prints and primitive toys. The symbolism of the ark as a place to find safety in the midst of chaos resonated with my life as a military wife. The ark reminded me of protection and rest, but the greatest reminder was that God had a plan, not only for me, but also for my family. I wrestled with the ramifications of rearing children who moved from one place to another versus the benefits of staying in one place. Captain and Mrs. Noah and their water bound quarters encouraged me to trust in God's plan and timing.

Scripture introduces Noah in Genesis 5, where we discover Noah was 500 years old when he became a parent, eventually to three boys. In a few short words, we find out about Noah and his character—he was righteous and blameless—two words that indicate Noah's wholehearted commitment to God.[1]

"Joan of Ark" is a common man-on-the-street response to the question, "Who was Noah's wife?" Wrong answer! Scripture provides limited information about Mrs. Noah. We know she held the status of a married woman who had sons, which was important in her day. We also know she endured over 100 years of her husband building an ark to prepare for a journey of a lifetime. This woman was a survivor. Along with her husband, her sons, and their wives, she survived the worst natural disaster ever recorded.[2]

Commonsense presumes that Captain and Mrs. Noah's three sons helped build the ark, fill the ark, and then care for the livestock they transported. God's call and plan was not just for Noah, but for his entire family.

When God called my husband to serve in the military—and yes, he saw it as a calling and not a job—he called our family. Each time we packed up to move, the Lord reminded me we were safe in the "ark" of his making. Captain and Mrs. Noah did not have to sacrifice their family to follow God's will. On the contrary, their family was the only one saved from the flood. God is also able to preserve and bless military families through the special calling of military service. Trust him to keep you and yours safe.

### Respond

How does the story of God's care for Noah's family encourage you as a mom rearing children in a military environment? In what ways do you see military life as a calling for your family?

### Prayer for the journey

Lord, thank you for your loving care for my family. Help me trust you to use the experiences of military life to bless my children. Show me that we are safe in the ark of your loving care today. Amen.

# Waypoint 2

*Letting God define your family values*

### Read

Now the earth was corrupt in God's sight, and the earth was filled with violence. And God saw the earth, and behold, it was corrupt, for all flesh had corrupted their way on the earth. And God said to Noah, "I have determined to make an end of all flesh, for the earth is filled with violence through them. Behold, I will destroy them with the earth." (Genesis 6:11–13)

If he did not spare the ancient world, but preserved Noah, a herald of righteousness, with seven others, when he brought a flood upon the world of the ungodly … then the Lord knows how to rescue the godly from trials, and to keep the unrighteous under punishment until the day of judgment. (2 Peter 2:5, 9)

### Reflect

In the many military moves our family made, one of the constant concerns was how our children would adjust to a new environment. One son made a mid-year first grade move. The other son experienced German school for three years, and then had to adjust to an American school. The transition to junior high and then to a different place for high school was especially difficult for both my boys. I worried whether they would find good friends. Would they be strong enough to say no to peer pressure or would the need to fit in cause them to exhibit negative behavior?

Our family had it easy compared to the Noah family. Their society was morally corrupt on a scale we cannot comprehend.

Did you notice how many times the words *corrupt* and *violence* are used in Genesis 6:11–13? The repeated use of those words tells us the corruption was not limited to a local area, but was widespread. Scripture informs us that sin was both extensive and intensive. The depravity of man was evident in both action and thought, so much so that God was grieved that he made man.[3] Sister, things could not get any worse.

In this corrupt setting we find Noah and his family. The words in 2 Peter 2:5 inform us that Noah was a "herald of righteousness." He warned people that God's judgment was coming. No one else got on the ark with Noah and his family, so obviously people did not believe his message. Neighbors could not ignore the big ark the family was building. They were most likely ridiculed and mocked as they walked through the marketplace. In today's world, people would know Noah's kids as the ones with the crazy father.

Through it all, Noah and his family stood against the rising tide of cultural immorality and committed to keeping their family values anchored in what was pleasing to God. Following the course their family took in navigating the culture of their day may be very relevant for us today when we consider the words of Jesus, "Just as it was in the days of Noah, so will it be in the days of the Son of Man" (Luke 17:26).

### Respond

What does the term "family values" mean to you? What are your most revered family values?

### Prayer for the journey

Lord, I pray the faith my children have in you will be strong enough to stand against the sway of culture. Help my husband and me to set an example of godliness as we live our lives trusting in you. Amen.

# Waypoint 3

*A family investment*

"Make yourself an ark of gopher wood. Make rooms in the ark, and cover it inside and out with pitch. This is how you are to make it: the length of the ark 300 cubits, its breadth 50 cubits, and its height 30 cubits. Make a roof for the ark, and finish it to a cubit above, and set the door of the ark in its side. Make it with lower, second, and third decks. For behold, I will bring a flood of waters upon the earth to destroy all flesh in which is the breath of life under heaven. Everything that is on the earth shall die. But I will establish my covenant with you, and you shall come into the ark, you, your sons, your wife, and your sons' wives with you." (Genesis 6:14–18)

Noah did this; he did all that God commanded him. (Genesis 6:22)

Reflect

Logistics Specialist 1st Class Reagan Pescoso and his wife are investment experts. I have no idea how much money they have in the bank, but they invest where it counts—in their family. Asked about parenting in the military, Pescoso said, "The hardest part about being in the military is spending time away from my family." When he is home from sea, he and his family cherish their time together. They invest time, energy, and resources in enjoying travel, playing board games, and finding interesting new places to eat together. The fulfilment and joy he finds in his family helps him cope when he is away. Twelve-year-old Lance Pescoso is proud of his dad's Navy service. He said, "I think it's cool he gets to go around the world helping people and supporting his country."[4]

Pescoso and his wife are making deposits in their family. "I hope my kids learn that their father did something big for our family by being in the military," Pescoso said. "I hope they learn to be better people because of it. I hope they learn from me how to be strong, patient, and value the importance of time with family."[5]

Dare we call Noah's family the first Navy family? As Noah prepared to embark on his voyage, he made an investment in time and resources. Genesis 6:22 says, *"Noah did ... "* The words emphasize Noah's obedience to God's instructions—he did what God told him to do. Scripture is silent about the effort and investment of such an undertaking. Think of the time and energy it took to cut the trees, deliver the trees, form the trees into planks, fit the planks, and then shape the planks into the ark. The monetary investment would have been enormous to provide food for the many animals they would carry.[6] Noah willingly made the investments, his family gathered everything they needed, and "the Lord shut [them] in" (Genesis 7:16).

God takes account of the investment you make in your family. Using God's Word as the blueprint for building a strong family will give you the confidence to know you are making a wise investment that leads to the saving of your family.

### Respond

What investments are you making in the spiritual lives of your children? How has military life made you more aware of your responsibility to make deposits into your family?

### Prayer for the journey

Lord, equip me as a parent with everything I need to do your will. Work in me what is pleasing to you. Help my husband and me to invest our time wisely with our children. May the deposits we make into their lives produce love for you. Amen.

# Waypoint 4

## *I used to be the perfect parent*

Noah began to be a man of the soil, and he planted a vineyard. He drank of the wine and became drunk and lay uncovered in his tent. And Ham, the father of Canaan, saw the nakedness of his father and told his two brothers outside. Then Shem and Japheth took a garment, laid it on both their shoulders, and walked backward and covered the nakedness of their father. Their faces were turned backward, and they did not see their father's nakedness." (Genesis 9:20–23)

I used to be the perfect parent—until I had children.

Honestly, I am so far from perfection, yet I place before me that standard. Crazy, right? Comparing our parenting skills (or lack thereof) with the countless Facebook status updates we read from friends and acquaintances leaves us feeling inadequate. Can I tell you something you can take to the bank? There are no perfect parents and no perfect kids.

A discussion on the website militaryspouse.com highlights some of the issues military moms struggle with concerning the need to be perfect:

My kids see me worrying about the next big change.

I have a hard time being positive around the kids.

I rely on my kids too much when my husband is deployed.

I hate to cook family meals, especially during deployments.

I try to be the perfect parent, and then burn out.[7]

Well, my perfection-seeking, never-hit-the-mark, fall-so-far-below-the-standard sister, I have good news for you! Remember the scriptural description of Noah as "righteous" and "blameless?" Remember that he was the only person in the world committed to God? Remember that he was a preacher of righteousness? Remember that God had such confidence in him that he put him in charge of the earth's do-over? Brace yourself—Noah was not perfect. He did not always act honorably. The account of saintly obedient Noah is in Genesis 6–8, but the account of drunken shameful Noah follows in Genesis 9.[8]

While not perfect, our imperfection is not a license to stop trying to be a good parent. When—not if—we make mistakes we can seek help from the Lord and, when appropriate, ask forgiveness from our family. The family of God lives on a healthy diet of mercy and grace. We should always give parenting our best effort, and trust the Lord to fill the gap when we fall short.

### Respond

Circle any areas below in which you struggle as a military parent:

- My kids see me worrying about the next big change.
- I have a hard time being positive around the kids.
- I rely on my kids too much when my husband is deployed.
- I hate to cook family meals, especially during deployments.
- I try to be the perfect parent, and then burn out.

Write a positive action step to address each of the statements above. Use these statements as a prayer guide.

### Prayer for the journey

Lord, only you are perfect. I confess to you the stress I allow myself to undergo in my effort toward perfection. Remind me when I fall short and feel inadequate to take my needs to you. In so doing, may I teach my children the power and peace of trusting you. Amen.

# Waypoint 5

## My three sons

> And God blessed Noah and his sons and said to them, "Be fruitful and multiply and fill the earth." (Genesis 9:1)

> Then God said to Noah and to his sons with him, "Behold, I establish my covenant with you and your offspring after you." (Genesis 9:8)

> These are the clans of the sons of Noah, according to their genealogies, in their nations, and from these the nations spread abroad on the earth after the flood. (Genesis 10:32)

### Reflect

My husband and I were invited to dinner at the home of a fellow military couple. They lived in historic military quarters—you know the kind where you wish the walls could talk? The walls did not need to talk to tell a fascinating story of family legacy. One of the first things my eyes fell upon when I entered the house was a horizontal collection of portraits of West Point cadets, which included our host. The photos displayed the family members who attended West Point for six consecutive generations dating back to 1823. The family represents one of the longest unbroken chains of West Point graduates. Obvious pride in the legacy of service has been passed down from one generation to the next.

Military families tend to pass down a legacy of service to their children. Approximately 79 percent (eight-in-ten) veterans have an immediate family member who served in the military.[9] The Military Child Education Coalition reports that children in military families are twice as likely as their civilian counterparts to join the military as adults.[10]

While military service is an honorable tradition to be associated with family heritage, nothing compares to the eternal legacy of passing on a steadfast faith in God. I am inspired and hopeful when I read God's promise in Genesis 9:8 that God made a covenant with Noah *and* his sons. As a parent, nothing would give me greater joy than knowing my children were committed to serving the Lord.

The ark was the means God used to save Noah and his family from the judgment of God. The ark is also a metaphor for all who are safe from God's eternal judgment through faith in the truth presented in God's Word. Whether you come from multi-generations of believers or you are the first believer in your family, you can look to the Lord to extend his mercy to your sons and daughters.

Along with the pride that accompanies an offspring filling a parent's military boots, we can also experience the peace that comes from knowing our children are in a right relationship with God. When we see our children serving the Lord, we know the meaning of the words of John, the disciple of Jesus, when he wrote, "I have no greater joy than to hear that my children are walking in the truth" (3 John 1:4).

### Respond

What steps are you taking to pass a legacy of faith to your children? In what ways is military life strengthening your legacy of faith?

### Prayer for the journey

Lord, help me to leave a spiritual legacy to my children. May my life and words tell of your glorious deeds, your might, and the wonders you have done. Amen. (See Psalm 78:4)

# Waypoint 6

*A place to hide*

Read

> Then Pharaoh commanded all his people, "Every son that is born to the Hebrews you shall cast into the Nile, but you shall let every daughter live." (Exodus 1:22)

> By faith Moses, when he was born, was hidden for three months by his parents, because they saw that the child was beautiful, and they were not afraid of the king's edict. (Hebrews 11:23)

Reflect

Imagine yourself pregnant. A "gender reveal" party is out of the question because your unborn baby may be a boy. You just want a healthy baby, but you pray this baby is not a boy. Why? The government has imposed a system of infanticide based on ethnicity, age, and gender, and you and your family fall into the target group.[11]

Amram and Jochebed, the parents of Moses, found themselves in such a predicament. An ordinary Israelite couple, they did not know the history of a nation rested on the way they would handle this crisis. How do you hide a baby?

Jewish families during World War II faced a similar predicament. The gut-wrenching stories of Hitler's systematic eradication of Jews left no more than 11 percent of Europe's pre-war Jewish population of children alive.[12] As the war progressed, many Jews sought to evade Hitler's henchmen by hiding their children. This difficult decision created major complications for parents. Where would they send the children for safety? How would they pay the often exorbitant fee for protection? More than not, Jewish parents who survived the war and reunited with their children reported severe psychological trauma that prohibited a return to normal family life.[13]

We do not have to go all the way back to World War II to see how the ravages of war still affect the innocent. Crises around our globe cause parents to flee in order to hide their children from the catastrophe of war. We in the United States rarely fathom such fear and loss. Too often, we are the ones who hide from the reality of what is going on in the rest of the world.

I know this is not a *feel good* devotional thought. I make no apologies. I ask that today, just for a moment, you bow your head and pray for the children who cannot hide from evil. Pray for parents who want safety and peace for their children. Pray for parents who hope and dream for a better future for their children. Then hug your child a little tighter and ask God to make us all change agents in a world longing for peace.

### Respond

If your children are old enough, consider reading together and discussing *The Hiding Place*, *The Diary of Anne Frank*, or *The Book Thief*. Do some research on agencies that are helping children displaced by war. Involve your children in finding a way to send financial support to one of these agencies.

### Prayer for the journey

Lord, I pray for children displaced because of war and violence. Provide shelter, sustenance, and protection. I pray for peace in lands ravaged by war. Show my family and me ways we can be a blessing and an agent of hope. Amen.

# Waypoint 7

*A beautiful child*

Read

Now a man from the house of Levi went and took as his wife a Levite woman. The woman conceived and bore a son, and when she saw that he was a fine child, she hid him three months (Exodus 2:1–2)

"But as the time of the promise drew near, which God had granted to Abraham, the people increased and multiplied in Egypt until there arose over Egypt another king who did not know Joseph. He dealt shrewdly with our race and forced our fathers to expose their infants, so that they would not be kept alive. At this time Moses was born; and he was beautiful in God's sight." (Acts 7:17–20a)

Reflect

If you are a parent, you no doubt remember the first time your eyes fell upon your child. The little scrunched-up wonder was beautiful to you. You knew this was no ordinary child.

I can imagine these same thoughts went through Jochebed's mind as she looked at Moses. In fact, enjoy this little-known piece of Bible trivia: Did you know Moses is the only baby described as beautiful in the Bible?[14]

My heart goes out to Jochebed as I envision her looking at her newborn boy. Times were tense. A new Pharaoh meant grave danger for her baby boy. Would he even have the opportunity to grow up and exercise his unique gifts, talents, and strengths?

My children share DNA, but they are different in temperament, looks, and abilities. The way my husband and I parent each of them is different. We work toward consistent principles, but their individual needs are different. For instance, during our PCS moves, one child would make friends quickly while the other one needed more time to adjust.

I look at each of my children and ask God to help me see and respect their unique qualities. How does that work its way out in every day living? Author Kenneth Boa suggests the recognition of individuality and dignity of each family member shows up through a positive and encouraging attitude. Boa elaborates:

> When people are sarcastic rather than supportive, re-
> lationships disintegrate. Since it takes about five posi-
> tive comments to overcome one negative remark, it is
> important for parents to be on their children's teams,
> not on their backs. They should avoid favoritism and
> comparisons of one child with another. It is especially
> important for parents to openly admit their mistakes
> and ask forgiveness from their children when they
> embarrass or insult them, break a promise, or mistreat
> them. In this way, honesty and esteem for each individ-
> ual become ingrained in the thinking of the children.[15]

Each of our children, created in the image of God, possesses their own unique beauty. Our job as parents is to help that beauty to blossom as they fulfill God's will for their lives.

## Respond

For each of your children, create a list of their unique characteristics, strengths, and talents. Use this list as a prayer guide for your children.

## Prayer for the journey

Lord, thank you for the unique gifts you placed within my children. Help me to always appreciate their individuality and celebrate their design. You formed them, and you know them. Give me wisdom to guide them in a direction that will allow them to discover and live out your will. Amen.

# Waypoint 8

*Moses in the bulrushes*

Read

> But when she could no longer hide him, she took an ark
> of bulrushes for him, daubed it with asphalt and pitch,
> put the child in it, and laid it in the reeds by the river's
> bank. (Exodus 2:3 NKJV)

Reflect

Baby Moses in the bulrushes is a popular children's Bible story. Never mind that no one can tell you what a bulrush is. The unbelievable part of the story highlights a mom preparing and placing her baby in a little floating basket to leave him on the bank of the Nile River. Who does that? The scene sounds counterintuitive for a mother who loves her child. Today, we would be calling Child Services on Jochebed, ASAP.

Jochebed's reason for making the little water bassinet was not for cruelty, but for love. At three months old, baby Moses discovered his voice and found that crying would bring food and cooing would bring attention. She could keep him hidden in her home no longer. Her love for this tiny fellow caused her to take drastic action to protect him from destruction. Perhaps no one would hear him cry inside the miniature ark. The sound of the water and the thickness of the covering would muffle any cry.[16] Perhaps she thought she could return to the ark among the bulrushes to nurse him.

I wonder if Jochebed was thinking of Noah and his ark when she constructed the vessel for baby Moses. Did she think about God's message of salvation to Noah and his household as she painted the inside and outside with pitch, just as Noah did years earlier? Perhaps this little ark would be a life preserver for her child as the huge ark was for Noah.

Scripture lists the word ark three different times: in reference to Noah, Moses, and the Ark of the Covenant in Exodus 25. All references point to salvation that can only come from God.[17] The reference rings true for Jochebed and her child.

There comes a time when I can no longer shield my children within the confines of my home. As much as I want to shelter them, I know at some point they must make their way in the world. I have no bulrushes to weave into an ark, and no pitch to seal the ark tight.

What I do have is the truth of God's Word to seal their minds from the deceptions of the world. I can brush it on in the morning and evening through family devotions, and apply it with prayer throughout the day, as needed for life's situations.

## Respond

What plan do you have for family devotions? If you do not have a plan, consider researching age-appropriate material and develop a family devotion strategy. If you do have a plan, how do you see it making a difference in the lives of your family members?

## Prayer for the journey

Lord, thank you for Jochebed's example of godly parenting. Help me to persevere in preparing my children for life outside our family home. Amen.

# Waypoint 9

*A parent's prayer*

Read

> His sister stood at a distance to see what would happen
> to him. Then Pharoah's daughter went down to the Nile
> to bathe, and her attendants were walking along the
> riverbank. She saw the basket among the reeds and sent
> her female slave to get it. She opened it and saw the baby.
> He was crying, and she felt sorry for him. "This is one of
> the Hebrew babies," she said. (Exodus 2:4–6 NIV)

Reflect

One of my prayers as a parent has been that God would
consistently intersect the lives of my children with people who
would point them toward his will for their lives. I pray for people
who can say things to them that they will hear and receive in
a way they may not hear and receive from me. God has been
faithful to answer this prayer over and over again.

I do not know all of the divine encounters my children have
experienced, but I remember one well. My son graduated from
high school, and after a year of college we received a call from
him with these words, "I feel like I am wasting my time and your
money." Grateful for his honesty, but concerned for his lack of
focus, my husband and I began to pray in earnest for God to
direct him. For over a year, he did some traveling, and then got
a job doing manual labor at barely minimum wage. He worked
with an older man who one day looked at him and said, "Son,
do you want to be doing what I'm doing when you're my age?"
My son responded, "With all due respect, no sir." The man said,
"Then you need to get yourself back in school and start working

toward a future." Soon after this conversation, my son returned to college and today is a successful middle school principal. I smile when I think of him today. Perhaps he is the answer to another parent's prayer as he intersects the lives of young people.

My husband's experience as a military chaplain serving with a basic training unit convinced him that God often uses drill sergeants to get young men and women back on the right track in life. After observing many physical, mental, and spiritual transformations of new recruits, he came to the conclusion that the drill sergeants were the catalysts for change, but the agent of change in a recruit was the Spirit of God moving in response to the prayers of families and churches back home.

I do not know if Jochebed prayed that someone would intersect her son's life, but it happened. Just as God orchestrated the events of Pharaoh's daughter bathing in the Nile River to influence the future of Moses, I believe God orchestrated the circumstances surrounding my son's working with a man who influenced his future. In God's great irony, the river that meant death and sorrow for Hebrew infants brought life and hope for Moses.[18] In that river, a mother's prayer and God's mercy intersected.

## Respond

Who were some of the people who intersected your life and pointed you to Christ? Consider writing a note of gratitude to them or pray for them asking God to bless them for their investment in your life.

## Prayer for the journey

Lord, I pray you would place in my child's life people who will point him/her to you. I pray your timing in divine appointments throughout the life of my child. I ask a blessing upon those people who take the time to speak life and hope to my child. Amen.

# Waypoint 10
*Jochebed's reward*

Read

> Then his sister asked Pharaoh's daughter, "Shall I go and get one of the Hebrew women to nurse the baby for you?" "Yes, go," she answered. So the girl went and got the baby's mother. Pharaoh's daughter said to her, "Take this baby and nurse him for me, and I will pay you." So the woman took the baby and nursed him. When the child grew older, she took him to Pharaoh's daughter and he became her son. She named him Moses, saying, "I drew him out of the water." (Exodus 2:7–10 NIV)

Reflect

Perhaps other mothers attempted to hide their children from Pharaoh's onslaught, but Scripture only gives us insight into the mother of Moses. Her diligent care and dangerous move resulted in great reward. Instead of turning her child over for death, Pharaoh's daughter rescued Moses and offered Jochebed the job of nursing him. Imagine the stress Jochebed felt during the days she tried to keep Moses quiet in her home. Finally, those days were over! Now she could freely interact with her child.

For seven years, she served as the caretaker of Moses in the house of Pharaoh. No doubt, she told Moses the stories of his Hebrew lineage and trained him in the ways of God. We do not know if she lived to see him deliver the Hebrews from bondage, but we do know her brave action set a divine plan in motion. Moses would grow up to rescue God's people from their slavery in Egypt.

Jochebed gave her son up to another and then God gave him back to her. Symbolically we do the same when we give our children to the Lord through baptism or dedication. In our military chapel in Germany, young couples would routinely present their babies to the Lord. In addition to receiving a pink or blue Bible and a certificate from the chapel, the Chaplain would take each child into his arms, pray and anoint him/her, and then give the child back to the parents. Through this act, the parents acknowledged their inability to provide for all their child's needs, and they put him or her into the hands of the only one who could, the Lord God Almighty.

God rewarded the trust and courage of Jochebed. Her actions spared her son from death and allowed her to remain a vital part of his life. The book of Hebrews does not list the parents of Moses by name, but their actions are listed among the heroes of faith in Hebrews 11:23, "By faith Moses, when he was born, was hidden for three months by his parents, because they saw that the child was beautiful, and they were not afraid of the king's edict."

### Respond

Jochebed trusted God with the life of her son and God rewarded her faith. In what ways do you trust God with your child/children? In what ways do you need to grow in trust?

### Prayer for the journey

Lord, help me to be a mother who lives by faith. So often, I try to maneuver situations and manipulate outcomes. Teach me how to entrust my child/children to you. Help me know you love and care for them more than I can imagine. Thank you for your great love. Amen.

# Waypoint 11

*The original 'mean girl'*

Read

There was a certain man of Ramathaim-zophim of the hill country of Ephraim whose name was Elkanah.... He had two wives. The name of the one was Hannah, and the name of the other, Peninnah. And Peninnah had children, but Hannah had no children. Now this man used to go up year by year from his city to worship and to sacrifice to the LORD of hosts at Shiloh ... On the day when Elkanah sacrificed, he would give portions to Peninnah his wife and to all her sons and daughters. But to Hannah he gave a double portion, because he loved her, though the Lord had closed her womb. And her rival used to provoke her grievously to irritate her, because the LORD had closed her womb. So it went on year by year. As often as she went up to the house of the LORD, she used to provoke her. (1 Samuel 1:1–7a)

Reflect

"Mean girl" is a pop culture term for bully. She is the girl who taunts and criticizes you, and may be nice to your face but vicious behind your back. You may think of encountering a mean girl only in junior high or high school, but mean girls emerge in every age bracket, every social status, in person and now online—and even in military spouse circles. A husband's rank, a spouse's involvement in the military community, child-rearing methods—all get their fair share of comments.[19]

In her book *Queen Bee Moms and Kingpin Dads*, Rosaline Wiseman attributes the motivation of mean girls to the desire to belong. Wiseman writes, "I realized I had underestimated how powerfully parents' social hierarchies influence how they guide their children's lives. *We don't leave cliques and peer pressure behind when we grow up or when we become parents; we just graduate to a new level with adults playing the roles.*"[20]

In the first chapter of 1 Samuel, we encounter one of the original mean girls. Peninnah was one of Elkanah's two wives. Remember, polygamy was a common practice in ancient Near Eastern culture, a culture that also measured a woman's worth by her ability to have children. As mean girls will, Peninnah took every opportunity to make Hannah, Elkanah's other wife, feel less-than. Peninnah used her children to elevate her own sense of superiority and lock Hannah out of the 'mommy clique.'

I humbly confess I have had my share of mean-girl moments. I have boasted about my child when someone else was struggling with hers. With self-righteousness, I have shared how my parenting tactic succeeded when someone else floundered. I did not set out to be unkind, and I prettied up my statements with spiritual words. On reflection, I am sure my mean-girl moments came from a place of insecurity and pride. I make excuses for my wrong behavior: hormones, personality differences, or having a bad day, but I have no valid excuse for what amounts to being a bully.

Sister, let's be on each other's team. Let's help each other be better wives, better moms, better women. Let's live the words of Ephesians 4:32: "Be kind to one another, tenderhearted, forgiving one another, as God in Christ forgave you."

### Respond

How can you put Ephesians 4:32 into action when you encounter mean-girl attitudes? What do you learn about kindness from Scripture (Luke 6:35; Colossians 3:12; Proverbs 31:10, 26)?

### Prayer for the journey

Lord, today may the teaching of kindness be on my tongue and in my actions. Amen.

# Waypoint 12

*An unhappy traveler*

> Therefore Hannah wept and would not eat. And Elkanah, her husband, said to her, "Hannah, why do you weep? And why do you not eat? And why is your heart sad? Am I not more to you than ten sons?" (1 Samuel 1:7b–8)

I have traveled with some people whose company I was less than thrilled to share. However, I have never traveled with anyone who deliberately taunted and provoked me like Peninnah did to Hannah. The trip to Shiloh was a yearly event that brought Hannah to tears and made her lose her appetite. She must have dreaded the journey to the feast each year, listening to Elkanah's fertile wife. I can hear Peninnah with an overly sarcastic tone going on and on about how perfect her children were, how favored she was to have children, how *very* sorry she was for *poor* Hannah. No wonder Hannah could not eat.

Hannah is one of many women in the Bible who struggled with infertility. If she lived today, statistics would inform her that she is among a group of over 10 percent of the population of child-bearing-age women. Even with today's medical knowledge, having to emotionally process the diagnosis of infertility can be devastating to a woman. At the time Hannah lived, society placed great expectations on wives. Those who could not have children were looked down upon, and in the case of Hannah, sometimes verbally ridiculed.

The journey Elkanah made with his family was to be a joyful journey.[21] For Hannah however, the trip only emphasized what she lacked. The question her husband Elkanah posed to her, "why is your heart sad?" is better translated, "why are you resentful and angry?"[22] A part of me wants to commend Elkanah for his obvious love for Hannah, but there is another part of me that wants to say, "Really?" I am not quite sure how to take his response, "Aren't I more valuable than ten sons?" I know he was trying to comfort her, but in my opinion, he missed the mark.

This time, family did not help. Peninnah deliberately pushed Hannah's hot button on motherhood and Elkanah, though he tried, did not really understand. Hannah internalized the pain she felt from the helplessness and hurt brought on by her situation.

To her credit, Hannah looked to the Lord for help. God opened her womb and gave her a son whom she would hold in her lap only a few short years until she sent him to grow up in the service of the Lord. God could have healed the hurt in Hannah's heart in a way other than the birth of a child. He knows what is best regarding all our personal struggles. Elkanah tried to bring his whole family together in worship, but Hannah needed something more. Just as the family altar is important today, it does not replace our personal relationship with, and devotion to the Lord. Hannah's hope did not come from anything other than her dependence upon her sovereign and faithful God.

### Respond

Read Psalm 13. What do you learn from this psalm about praying when things are difficult and challenging? How might this psalm translate into a prayer for someone struggling with infertility? Pray this prayer today for someone who is having a hard time becoming a parent.

### Prayer for the journey

Lord, "I have trusted in your steadfast love; my heart shall rejoice in your salvation. I will sing to the Lord, because he has dealt bountifully with me" (Psalm 13:5–6). Amen.

# Waypoint 13

*A prayer meeting in the temple*

Read

> After they had eaten and drunk in Shiloh, Hannah rose. Now Eli the priest was sitting on the seat beside the doorpost of the temple of the LORD. She was deeply distressed and prayed to the LORD and wept bitterly. And she vowed a vow and said, "O LORD of hosts, if you will indeed look on the affliction of your servant and remember me and not forget your servant, but will give to your servant a son, then I will give him to the LORD all the days of his life, and no razor shall touch his head" (1 Samuel 1:9–11).

## Reflect

My sadness for Hannah turns to respect as I read more of her story. Hannah decided she had felt sorry for herself long enough. She took her anger, bitterness, and discontent to God in prayer. The day she stopped to have a prayer meeting in the temple was a day that changed her life forever. She did not make a deal with God, manipulate him, or force him to bless her. No, she left her desperation at the altar, broke a cycle of despair, and rose up with newfound hope. Hannah spent years feeling that God was silent, but that day she rose from prayer with the words of a prophet spoken over her, *"'Go in peace, and the God of Israel grant your petition that you have made to him.' And she said, 'Let your servant find favor in your eyes.' Then the woman went her way and ate, and her face was no longer sad"* (1 Samuel 1:17–18).

In her desperation, she made a vow to God. If God would give her a son, she would give him back to God for service. Her request that God *remember* her was more than a reminder to God of her existence; she was pleading with him to act on her behalf.[23]

Sister, does anything make you feel desperate today? Do you feel like the constant adjustments of military life are going to mess up your kids? Do you struggle to feel *adequate* in the sea of perceived *perfect* moms? Are you exhausted as you await a deployed husband's return? Do you feel like you are swimming upstream in your effort to keep your preteen or teen on the right path? Oh friend, can I tell you that God remembers you? Be encouraged as you read the rest of Hannah's story. She left that prayer meeting and traveled home with her husband. Scripture says, "the LORD remembered her. And in due time Hannah conceived and bore a son, and she called his name Samuel, for she said, 'I have asked for him from the LORD'" (1 Samuel 1:19b–20).

Do not hesitate to call on the Lord. Regardless of what you face, spend time in prayer talking with God about the things that trouble you. The Word of God encourages us to cast all our cares on the Lord, because he cares for us (1 Peter 5:7). Did you notice in the Scripture recorded that when Hannah left the presence of the Lord, she ate some food and her face was no longer sad? She had not given birth, nor had she conceived. Yet in her heart, her faith had conceived the promise of God, and in due time the promise was born.

## Respond

In her desperation, Hannah turned to God instead of away from him. What does that tell you about her? To whom or what do you turn when you feel disappointment?

## Prayer for the journey

Lord, I sometimes find it too easy to take comfort in things that are not emotionally or spiritually healthy. Thank you for the example of Hannah, who took her disappointment to you. Help me to put my faith in you, no matter the circumstances. Amen.

# Waypoint 14

*No worthless women here!*

> As she continued praying before the LORD, Eli observed her mouth. Hannah was speaking in her heart; only her lips moved, and her voice was not heard. Therefore Eli took her to be a drunken woman. And Eli said to her, "How long will you go on being drunk? Put your wine away from you." But Hannah answered, "No, my lord, I am a woman troubled in spirit. I have drunk neither wine nor strong drink, but I have been pouring out my soul before the LORD. Do not regard your servant as a worthless woman, for all along I have been speaking out of my great anxiety and vexation." (1 Samuel 1:12–16)

Reflect

Let's revisit that prayer meeting in the temple. While she was praying, Hannah caught the eye of Eli, the priest. As Eli watched her, he thought she was drunk. However, Hannah was not pouring out drinks to abate her sorrow, she was pouring out her soul to God in prayer.[24] Now comes one of my favorite scenes: Eli confronted Hannah with his assumption of drunkenness. She did not make excuses for her actions, nor did she lower her head in shame or embarrassment for being mistakenly deemed drunk. Instead, she honestly stated her situation and then made this powerful statement: *"Do not regard your servant as a worthless woman."* Such boldness is not what I would expect from a woman who has been told she is worthless on a regular basis.

I have not experienced the desperation of barrenness or the incessant taunting of mean girls. My desperation has come from my own negative self-talk and the lies I willingly believed about myself and my ability to parent. The messages: "You are going to ruin your child … you are a terrible mother" have often reverberated in my mind. If I had been Hannah that day in the temple, I would have looked at Eli and said, "Yes, I am a worthless woman."

Thank God, Hannah did not let her situation define her. Instead, she looked to God and held on to him in her time of sorrow. She found her worth in God. Take the time to read 1 Samuel 2 and be inspired by the words of Hannah's prayer. She is the first and only woman in the Bible to speak a prayer and have it quoted in Scripture for us to read.[25] Her prayer is one of a woman who knows God's strength and power firsthand. She is one who persisted in prayer when it looked like nothing would change her condition.

God used Hannah to birth one of Israel's godliest prophets. Her son Samuel would anoint and mentor Israel's first kings.[26] God delights in birthing greatness from the womb of despair. Only God knows the true value of an eternal soul. Even those who others assume as worthless, from a human estimation, God has validated worthy by sending his Son to redeem them. In God's evaluation, they are priceless!

### Respond

Read Hannah's prayer in 1 Samuel 2:1–10 and list what you learn about Hannah's belief in God.

### Prayer for the journey

Lord, I praise you with the words of Hannah: *"There is none holy like the LORD; for there is none besides you; there is no rock like [my] God!"* (1 Samuel 2:2). Because of Jesus, you call me worthy. I stand forever grateful. Amen.

# Waypoint 15
## *For this child I prayed*

### Read

"For this child I prayed, and the LORD has granted me my petition that I made to him. Therefore I have lent him to the LORD. As long as he lives, he is lent to the LORD." (1 Samuel 1:27–28)

Samuel was ministering before the LORD, a boy clothed with a linen ephod. And his mother used to make for him a little robe and take it to him each year when she went up with her husband to offer the yearly sacrifice. Then Eli would bless Elkanah and his wife, and say, "May the LORD give you children by this woman for the petition she asked of the LORD." So then they would return to their home. (1 Samuel 2:18–20)

### Reflect

When I read Hannah's story I think of the many military wives who have sent not only a husband to war, but a child as well. A parent's concern for a child's safety does not end—no matter the age. Such concern was the impetus for a group of mothers to come together during World War II to form the Blue Star Mothers of America. This organization continues to provide support to parents with children in military service. The name originated from the Service Banner with blue stars hung in the window of a home. Each star represented a family member serving in war.[27]

One military wife and mom I know sent her Ranger husband off on dangerous assignments many times. Today her oldest son has been in some challenging situations as an Army Military Intelligence officer and her youngest son serves with the Air

Force's Special Operations team. She said, "It feels different to have your children go through dangerous and difficult training and then be sent down range. I was always concerned for my husband, but I felt like he could take care of himself. My mother's heart is inclined to protect and shelter my kids, no matter what age. I know my children serving in the military are very much the subjects of my prayers. I also know that their need for prayer has blessed our family in keeping us united in our concern for them."

Hannah did not make and hang a Blue Star Service Banner in her window to indicate the service of her son in the temple. She used her sewing skills to make a robe she carried to him each year, demonstrating her love and concern. The robes met little Samuel's need for clothing and warmth. Yet the robes symbolized so much more. They reminded Hannah of God's answer to her desperate prayer and were a witness to the Lord that she had been faithful in keeping her promise to him. No doubt, Samuel was reassured that his mother thought of him often and loved him very much. I can also imagine that Hannah told Samuel something like, "Every day when you put on this robe, remember how special you are to me and to God. You are a blessing!"

The Bible does not record how many years Hannah brought Samuel a new robe. I would guess as long as she was able. How long do we hold our children up before the Lord in prayer? Let's continue as long as we can formulate a thought and take a breath.

### Respond

The robes Hannah made for Samuel were a symbol of answered prayer. What might be a symbol of answered prayer for you as a parent? What are ways you communicate to your child the blessing from God they are to you?

### Prayer for the journey

Lord, help me find ways throughout the day to share the blessing my children are to me. Thank you for the gift of children. Amen.

# Waypoint 16
*'Why?' or 'How?'*

In the sixth month the angel Gabriel was sent from God to a city of Galilee named Nazareth, to a virgin betrothed to a man whose name was Joseph, of the house of David. And the virgin's name was Mary. And he came to her and said, "Greetings, O favored one, the Lord is with you!" But she was greatly troubled at the saying, and tried to discern what sort of greeting this might be. And the angel said to her, "Do not be afraid, Mary, for you have found favor with God. And behold, you will conceive in your womb and bear a son, and you shall call his name Jesus. He will be great and will be called the Son of the Most High. And the Lord God will give to him the throne of his father David, and he will reign over the house of Jacob forever, and of his kingdom there will be no end." (Luke 1:26–33)

## Reflect

Too often, I view the story of the angel visiting Mary to foretell the birth of Jesus as a sweet Christmas story. However, when I reflect on the magnitude of this event, the story moves from sweet to monumental. Consider the major ramifications this announcement would have on Mary's relationship with her fiancé, not to mention the way her society would view her when she became pregnant without being married.

How many of us, after getting over the shock of an angelic visitation would second guess the message and start mulling over the cost to our reputation? I am quite sure my response would have been, "Why me?" in the voice of a victim rather than a humble, willing servant of God. Thank goodness, young Mary did not respond that way. Mary embraced God's will for her life and for her future family. She did not ask, "Why me?" No, she asked, "How can this be?"

An angel's journey from God's heavenly realm to inform Mary of her destiny began her unprecedented pilgrimage of obedience. She had the choice to respond with "Why me?" or "How can this be?" I have thought long and hard about the difference between the two responses, and I conclude that asking "Why me?" makes me a victim, but asking, "How can this be?" makes me a participant in God's plan.

As a military mom, I have that same choice when issues arise. I can choose to ask, "Why me?" when challenges of military life seem overwhelming. I confess, at times I make that choice and I must tell you it does not get me anywhere but into a hole of self-pity. However, when I choose to ask, "How can this be?" I become energized by the challenge of trusting God with the possibilities of the future.

Mary's situation had the component of God's divine will as she fulfilled her part of the plan in birthing the Savior of the world. Sister, God has a will and plan for your family. He has a plan, but we must be willing to participate. Are you willing to say, "How can this be?"

## Respond

Are you more of a, "Why me?" or "How can this be?" person? How might each response have an effect on parenting?

## Prayer for the journey

Lord, forgive me when I have had a victim mentality and cried, "Why me?" Help me to always look for possibilities as I trust you for the future. Amen.

# Waypoint 17

*When you need to be with family*

### Read

> In those days Mary arose and went with haste into the hill country, to a town in Judah, and she entered the house of Zechariah and greeted Elizabeth. And when Elizabeth heard the greeting of Mary, the baby leaped in her womb. And Elizabeth was filled with the Holy Spirit, and she exclaimed with a loud cry, "Blessed are you among women, and blessed is the fruit of your womb!" (Luke 1:39–40)

### Reflect

A visit to grandparents and a special aunt and uncle became a retreat for my boys and me during my husband's deployments and TDY (Temporary Duty) assignments. I would pack up our gear and we would head south. Often, the prescription to get through a month was the support and solace offered by family. When I needed help with my children, they offered extra hands. When I needed a spot to rest and recuperate from the frenetic activity of my community, they offered space. When I needed to be reminded of my place in the family, they offered roots. When I missed my husband, they offered comfort.

Scripture does not tell us why Mary chose to visit Elizabeth. We know the angel informed Mary that Elizabeth was pregnant. Such news had to get Mary's attention because the description of Elizabeth in Luke 1 was that she was barren and "advanced in years." Mary knew she was not the only one experiencing a miracle!

Even with such knowledge, I wonder if Mary worried whether Elizabeth might send her home when she saw Mary's condition. Or did she know Elizabeth and Zechariah would offer her the support and needed space to process what was happening? Fortunately, Elizabeth's welcome was without question. Upon hearing Mary's greeting Elizabeth spoke the words, "Blessed are you among women, and blessed is the child you will bear!" You can almost hear Mary's sigh of relief. As an unmarried pregnant woman, she could have been stoned, or at least disgraced, but Elizabeth offered blessing.

Notice that Mary did not go to Elizabeth with whines, sighs, and commiseration. She did not visit her family to hide from ridicule or escape responsibility. Mary expressed the joy of knowing she was helping to fulfill God's plan for the world. No doubt she and Elizabeth shared their questions, discomforts, and amazement as confidantes and participants in a "mysterious mission."[28]

There are times when you need support from your extended family. During a deployment, or when a service member is unavailable, can be an appropriate time to look to family members for help. Needing support is not a sign of weakness. In fact, it can become an opportunity for the extended family to participate in your service to the nation.

God was working in Elizabeth in a special way that provided mutual encouragement and support for her and Mary. God can work in your extended family during a period to encourage and offer practical help for you as well.

### Respond

How has your extended family supported your military family? Perhaps your family cannot be relied upon for support. How have you reached out to create a surrogate extended family?

### Prayer for the journey

Lord, thank you for friends and family who are willing to help in times of need. I am grateful for people who love and care for me and my family. Show me ways I can be a help and blessing to them as well. Amen.

# Waypoint 18

*Treasures of the heart*

Read

> When the angels went away from them into heaven, the shepherds said to one another, "Let us go over to Bethlehem and see this thing that has happened, which the Lord has made known to us." And they went with haste and found Mary and Joseph, and the baby lying in a manger. And when they saw it, they made known the saying that had been told them concerning this child. And all who heard it wondered at what the shepherds told them. But Mary treasured up all these things, pondering them in her heart. And the shepherds returned, glorifying and praising God for all they had heard and seen, as it had been told them. (Luke 2:15–20)

## Reflect

I looked out the window and noticed my five-year-old son taking charge of the neighborhood children gathered in our military housing yard. More than one of my friends pointed out his future as a military leader at best, or dictator at worst. He did not become either one, but others who saw leadership potential in my son encouraged me. Teachers and employers continue to affirm and develop his leadership skills. As his mom, I have pondered, prayed, and at times puzzled over how the pieces of his life would fit together to fulfill the potential I saw in that assertive five-year-old boy.

There in Bethlehem, Mary sat with her newborn baby. Sitting in that stable, did she wonder if the visit from the angel that told her she would birth the Messiah was a dream? Did she look around and think, "How can the Savior of the world be born here? I must have misunderstood the message." Just then, a motley crew of shepherds showed up with the news that angels had told them where to find the baby—another angelic visitation bringing confirmation that her child indeed was special.

Do not be fooled to think that the words, "But Mary treasured up all these things, pondering them in her heart" is the equivalent of creating a sentimental Hallmark image. This young mom was not sweetly capturing a moment in the scrapbook of her mind. No, she was grappling with the facts and striving to "pull it all together."[29] She intellectually and emotionally analyzed the information. Her *pondering* was not a meditative exercise, but a prayerful and determined wrestling with the possibilities of what was happening. She wanted to glean the truth about her child.[30]

Sometimes accurately evaluating the abilities and potential of our own children is challenging. Being a grandparent challenges this even more. Though we never want to let anyone define our children's capabilities or determine their potential, we can be encouraged when others see the same good qualities in our children that we see. God can use others either to confirm what we think we see, or to notice some aspect of potential greatness that we have not yet noticed.

### Respond

List the strengths you see in your child/children. What are you *treasuring* and *pondering* about your child/children right now?

### Prayer for the journey

Create a prayer for your child/children from the strengths list you created.

# Waypoint 19

*Band of mothers*

Read

> And when the time came for their purification according to the Law of Moses, they brought him up to Jerusalem to present him to the Lord. (Luke 2:22)

> Now there was a man in Jerusalem, whose name was Simeon, and this man was righteous and devout, waiting for the consolation of Israel, and the Holy Spirit was upon him. And it had been revealed to him by the Holy Spirit that he would not see death before he had seen the Lord's Christ. (Luke 2:25–26)

> And there was a prophetess, Anna, the daughter of Phanuel, of the tribe of Asher. She was advanced in years, having lived with her husband seven years from when she was a virgin, and then as a widow until she was eighty-four. She did not depart from the temple, worshiping with fasting and prayer night and day. And coming up at that very hour she began to give thanks to God and to speak of him to all who were waiting for the redemption of Jerusalem. (Luke 2:36–38)

Reflect

This week I was introduced to the son of a good friend and fellow military wife. Her introduction of me to her son ended with, "She prays for you." I had never met this young man, but I have prayed for him often—for a job, a relationship, a home, and most importantly, salvation. I remember the day a text came through from this mom about her son's baptism and declaration of faith. What a day of rejoicing for answered prayer! The introduction reminded me of the dear military friends who have become like family to me. One sweet circle of friends has become known as the "Praying Aunties." As the family of God, we have invested in each other's children through our prayers.

The journey from Bethlehem to Jerusalem to fulfill the law of purification presents Mary and Joseph as faithful parents.[31] As they entered the temple to make their offering, they encountered two elderly strangers who offered words of blessing over Jesus. Simeon and Anna were what I describe as *prayer warriors*. These godly prophets were regular fixtures at the temple who prayed and awaited the arrival of the Messiah. Their prayer life was obviously in tune with the Spirit of God, for they both recognized Jesus as the Messiah when Mary and Joseph entered the temple.

Once again, this family received confirmation that the strange events surrounding the birth of Jesus were not imagined. They must have found encouragement and hope as they listened to the blessing and prophecy concerning their child. This had to be a spiritual marker in their unusual parenting journey.

Anna and Simeon devoted their lives to praying in the temple for the Messiah to come. They watched for that special child who would grow up to be the Savior. Perhaps they placed a hand on the head and prayed for each child they touched. What a gift to a parent! If you pray for my child, you endear yourself to me! A more powerful group than a Band of Brothers who fights together for their nation is a Band of Mothers who prays together for their children.

Respond

Who are people who pray for your children? Write a note of gratitude to them today. How can you band together with other moms to pray for your children?

Prayer for the journey

List the names of your friends' children and pray for them today.

# Waypoint 20

*Military brat*

> Now when they had departed, behold, an angel of the
> Lord appeared to Joseph in a dream and said, "Rise, take
> the child and his mother, and flee to Egypt, and remain
> there until I tell you, for Herod is about to search for the
> child, to destroy him." And he rose and took the child
> and his mother by night and departed to Egypt and
> remained there until the death of Herod. This was to
> fulfill what the Lord had spoken by the prophet, "Out
> of Egypt I called my son." (Matthew 2:13–15)

Reflect

I used to balk when my children were given the moniker *Military
Brat* until I learned the origin of the term. It is derived from the
British Army and, like so many military terms, *brat* refers to
BRAT—an acronym that stands for British Regiment Attached
Traveler. When a member of the British Army received an
accompanied overseas assignment, the military issued BRAT
status to the family. Over the years wives objected to the term,
but the name stuck in reference to children.[32]

Overseas assignments can be bittersweet events for a
military family. On the sweet side are the opportunities for
broadening experiences. My own children became more
adaptable, empathetic, supportive, and creative because they
lived in other countries. On the bitter side, we spent several
years far away from family, and dealt with the stressful unknown
expectations that come with living in a foreign culture.

My family adjusted to life on the other side of each ocean.
My husband had accompanied tours of duty in both Germany

and Korea. I know what it means to drive through streets and think, "This is a nice place to visit," only to remember it would be my home for several years. I am still not crazy about calling my children *military brats*, but I am grateful for the experience the military afforded our family to travel abroad as we fulfilled God's plan for our lives.

The family of Jesus experienced their first foreign PCS when he was a young child. The move to Egypt was not to serve in the military but to save Jesus from death by Herod's military. As with military families, they went to Egypt for a limited time and later returned to their home in Nazareth. Nevertheless, for a season, they faced cultural challenges and language barriers as they confronted the reality of living in a foreign culture.

Even though Mary and Joseph moved to a foreign country to escape an enemy threat, the move was a God ordained, blessed, and watched-over event. The PCS to Egypt was all part of God's plan for them. Mary and Joseph may not have been able to see it at that point, but their move was a fulfillment of an Old Testament prophecy from Hosea 11:1, *"When Israel was a child, I loved him, and out of Egypt I called my son."*

God has a plan for you and your military family too. In every assignment, in whatever country, look for ways God wants to work in you and use you in his service. He can take every experience and make something meaningful out of it—for your good and for his glory.

### Respond

What concerns do you have about your child being a Military BRAT? What comfort do you find in knowing God's plan for your husband's military service includes you and your children?

### Prayer for the journey

Use the list of concerns you wrote about your child being a Military BRAT as your prayer prompt today.

# Waypoint 21

*The sweet spot*

Read

Now his parents went to Jerusalem every year at the Feast of the Passover. And when he was twelve years old, they went up according to custom. And when the feast was ended, as they were returning, the boy Jesus stayed behind in Jerusalem. His parents did not know it, but supposing him to be in the group they went a day's journey, but then they began to search for him among their relatives and acquaintances, and when they did not find him, they returned to Jerusalem, searching for him. After three days they found him in the temple, sitting among the teachers, listening to them and asking them questions. And all who heard him were amazed at his understanding and his answers. And when his parents saw him, they were astonished. And his mother said to him, "Son, why have you treated us so? Behold, your father and I have been searching for you in great distress." And he said to them, "Why were you looking for me? Did you not know that I must be in my Father's house?" (Luke 2:41–49)

Reflect

Don't you love it when your child finds their sweet spot—that thing that holds their attention and piques their interest? In our family, one child has an insatiable interest in factoids. He enjoys reading books about unusual facts and is a trove of trivia knowledge. Another child finds great joy in figuring out how things work. He will take apart and put together anything that does not move.

The yearly journey to Jerusalem for Passover is another indicator of Joseph and Mary's devotion to God. The dangerous trip took three or four days—an obvious sacrifice of time and resources for a carpenter's family,[33] but taking Jesus to the annual celebration was a step in his religious education.[34] The temple was not only a place of worship, but also a place of learning as evidenced by the teachers who were present. Here we have only a snapshot of his education, but the scene indicates the parents of Jesus were involved in his training. In the temple, Jesus lingered, listened, and entered into discussion with the teachers.

When they realized Jesus was not with them, they went into panic mode. After an anxious three-day search, they found him in his sweet spot—in the temple, talking with the teachers. He had a thirst and aptitude to discuss spiritual issues. His parents sound more annoyed than astounded, angry not about the learning but because Jesus stayed behind without permission.

As the Son of God, Jesus is different from other kids, but all kids have individual interests and needs. Even though military families move around, we can still address the unique educational needs of our children. I recently met one energetic military mom with five children in five different schools! Nicole's situation is unusual—and challenging, but she recognizes the temporary nature of her educational taxi service. She is dedicated to helping her children find their sweet spot. The prayer she and her husband pray for their kids uses the words at the end of this story about Jesus in the temple: May they increase *"in wisdom and in stature and in favor with God and man"* (Luke 2:52).

## Respond
What do you see as your child's sweet spots? How are you helping your children find them?

## Prayer for the journey
Lord, I pray _____ will increase "in wisdom, in stature and in favor with God and man." Amen.

# Waypoint 22

*When there's no place like home*

> On the third day there was a wedding at Cana in Galilee, and the mother of Jesus was there. Jesus also was invited to the wedding with his disciples. When the wine ran out, the mother of Jesus said to him, "They have no wine." And Jesus said to her, "Woman, what does this have to do with me? My hour has not yet come." His mother said to the servants, "Do whatever he tells you."
> (John 2:1–5)

Reflect

*"Abrupt!"*

*"I feel like someone chopped off an appendage!"*

*"There's no place like home. No, really—there's NO place like home!"*

The statements above describe my emotions when my family moved from North Carolina to Washington D.C. at the same time my oldest son left home to attend college in Tennessee. The transition felt brusque and harsh to me. Over the next few months we adjusted to D.C. as our new home, but when our son came to D.C. on school holidays he felt like he was visiting a strange city.

The shift from being supervisor of daily activities to mentor of an adult child is a necessary and natural adjustment for parents and children. However, the change in roles can feel curt for military families when home base suddenly changes to an unfamiliar location.

Mary had to feel some of the same emotions as her parenting role shifted. After all, how do you parent the Son of God? No miracles are recorded in the New Testament up to the miracle described in John chapter two, but this was the beginning of the public ministry of Jesus. Jesus performed this miracle at the prompting of his mother. Things would not be the same after this miraculous event.

The response of Jesus to Mary's request may seem harsh to our Western way of thinking, but when Jesus addressed Mary as *"woman,"* he took the necessary step toward redefining their roles. His identity moved from son to Savior. He was not only the son of Mary; he was also the Son of God. He willingly responded to her request to do something to help the bride and groom, but he did not do it under her authority. This time he moved in the authority granted him by God.[35] Mary's response was exemplary. She did not take offense, question him, or rebuke him for his response to her. She trusted him to do the right thing, illustrated by her command, *"Do whatever he tells you."*

Whether the adjustment is a swift ninety-degree turn or a slow curve, remember that parents still play an important role as children leave home. Your role as one who believes and trusts in our children's God given talents and gifts will not change. Your encouragement can be your child's *home*, no matter where you live.

### Respond

How was your experience when you left home for the first time? In what ways would you want it to be the same or different for your child?

### Prayer for the journey

Pray for someone you know who sent a child to college this year. Let them know you prayed for them today.

# Waypoint 23

*Where are you from?*

Read

> While he was still speaking to the people, behold, his mother and his brothers stood outside, asking to speak to him. But he replied to the man who told him, "Who is my mother, and who are my brothers?" And stretching out his hand toward his disciples, he said, "Here are my mother and my brothers! For whoever does the will of my Father in heaven is my brother and sister and mother." (Matthew 12:46–50)

Reflect

Ask either of my boys where they are from and the answer will be, "Nowhere." I know this because I posed the question to each of them. I also asked them if they resented the day they had to turn in their military ID card after they reached the age of ineligibility. My guilt was assuaged when they both answered, "No."

As I spent time on a Military BRAT web forum I learned that many adults who grew up in a military family struggle with a sense of belonging well after they relinquish their ID. One woman wrote of her experience, "We no longer carry a Military ID, and we are no longer welcomed on a military installation. In fact, the military does not even recognize our existence. They have taken our privileges, and we are left to ourselves to adapt to a foreign, civilian world. The second we resign our ID card, we resign our identity."[36]

When Jesus asked the question, "Who is my mother, and who are my brothers?" he was not denying his relationship with his family. Rather, he pointed out that from an eternal perspective his family included all of those who live for God. In a practical sense, he was showing the transition from his identity being from his family of origin to his disciples partnering with him in ministry. Jesus established a community in which believing on him as Savior means we are all "accepted in the beloved" (Ephesians 1:6 KJV).

As military families, we must prepare our children for the day they leave the nest. That preparation must include a thorough understanding of our confidence in their unique ability to contribute to the world. Most importantly, that preparation must include an understanding of their identity as a child of God. Their military ID card may expire, but their status as residents of God's Kingdom will bring a sense of belonging that a military ID cannot begin to match.

### Respond

In what ways are you preparing your child to leave the nest? In what ways are you teaching your child about their identity in Christ?

### Prayer for the journey

Lord, I pray my child would know your great love. Help my child to grow up to experience your grace and mercy in abundance. Amen.

# Waypoint 24

*A mother lion awakened!*

And when Jesus had finished these parables, he went away from there, and coming to his hometown he taught them in their synagogue, so that they were astonished, and said, "Where did this man get this wisdom and these mighty works? Is not this the carpenter's son? Is not his mother called Mary? And are not his brothers James and Joseph and Simon and Judas? And are not all his sisters with us? Where then did this man get all these things?" And they took offense at him. But Jesus said to them, "A prophet is not without honor except in his hometown and in his own household." And he did not do many mighty works there, because of their unbelief. (Matthew 13:53–58)

## Reflect

Do you remember the first time someone rejected or treated your child poorly? I sure do! The strong emotions of anger mixed with compassion and an overwhelming need to protect my child welled up within me. Someone had to hold me back and talk me down! The mother lion in me was awakened and I was ready to pounce on those who mistreated my cub.

My kids experienced the spectrum of acceptance and its lack because of their military status. At Ft. Leavenworth they attended a great school on the installation. They met acceptance from the other kids because all the kids were military like them. When we moved to North Carolina they attended a public school. My youngest son began playing on the varsity football team as a sophomore. However, when the coach found out that we would be moving in the middle of the season he pulled him out of play. The coach rejected him because he was a military kid who would not be around next year to help the team. Yeah, someone had to hold me back and talk me down after that situation!

Was Mary like me when Jesus was rejected in his hometown? Jesus did not follow the pattern of hometown boys. Surely a good Jewish boy would have remained in the village and continued his father's occupation as a carpenter. Add in that Jesus was teaching beyond what the townsfolk thought was his ability and you get rejection. He did not fit their preconceived ideas of a homeboy.[37] Their inflexibility and unbelief was their loss, because "he did not do many mighty works" among them.

As a mother, I must look at the big picture. Was I angry and disappointed for my child when he was rejected because of his dad's job? Yes. Did I think it was unfair? Yes. (It was!) However, disappointments and, yes, even rejection, can prepare and train kids for the realities of a world that can be unfair and harsh. My natural tendency is to get angry, protect, and strike back. But I need to remember that I am not rearing children, I am rearing adults. Handled wisely, rejection can build resilience and character. Our children need to learn how to bounce back in spite of challenges. Military kids can grow up to be resilient adults.

## Respond

What difference does it make to think of your role as rearing adults as opposed to rearing children? How have you helped your child bounce back from challenges?

## Prayer for the journey

Lord, help me to have a spirit of resilience when challenges come my way. I pray I will be an example to my child/children. Help our family to trust you in times of uncertainty, fear, or change. Amen.

# Waypoint 25

*Families take care of each other*

> [B]ut standing by the cross of Jesus were his mother and his mother's sister, Mary the wife of Clopas, and Mary Magdalene. When Jesus saw his mother and the disciple whom he loved standing nearby, he said to his mother, "Woman, behold, your son!" Then he said to the disciple, "Behold, your mother!" And from that hour the disciple took her to his own home. (John 19:25–27)

Reflect

I cannot begin to grasp the sadness, fear, and grief Mary must have felt as she watched Jesus journey to the cross. Her son—her firstborn—was fighting his most significant battle to accomplish the ultimate victory for mankind. The battle with spiritual and physical forces weakened him to the point of total exhaustion. His suffering was beyond comprehension. Yet surrounded by political authorities and bystanders who demanded his death, he showed concern for his mother.

This scene at the cross exemplifies the strength of family ties and the responsibility we have to care for each other even during the most difficult times. Jesus knew that after his death and resurrection, he would no longer continue as Mary's son in the flesh, but her human needs for care would remain. He assigned the disciple he loved the role of caregiver.

Her grief was palpable, but for her this was not the end. As you read the first chapter of the book of Acts, you will discover that Mary was waiting in the Upper Room with all who had gathered for the promised Holy Spirit to come. She was present at the formation of the church as described in Acts 1:14: "All these with one accord were devoting themselves to prayer, together with the women and Mary the mother of Jesus, and his brothers." She would continue to claim and proclaim Jesus as Messiah and Lord. The same Holy Spirit, who overshadowed her when the angel came and told her she would give birth to Jesus, would fill her with power to carry on the mission of Jesus after his resurrection.[38]

Jesus shows us how we can fulfill our individual calling in life, while expressing an appropriate level of concern for others in our family and doing what we can to meet their needs.

### Respond

In what ways does your family take care of each other? No matter the age of your child, it is never too soon to think about the future. How do you want to be cared for as you grow older?

### Prayer for the journey

Lord, I pray the faith of my family would grow strong. I pray we would see your hand in this day and find you in the details of life. Amen.

# Waypoint 26

*Persistence pays off*

And Jesus went away from there and withdrew to the district of Tyre and Sidon. And behold, a Canaanite woman from that region came out and was crying, "Have mercy on me, O Lord, Son of David; my daughter is severely oppressed by a demon." But he did not answer her a word. And his disciples came and begged him, saying, "Send her away, for she is crying out after us." He answered, "I was sent only to the lost sheep of the house of Israel." But she came and knelt before him, saying, "Lord, help me." And he answered, "It is not right to take the children's bread and throw it to the dogs." She said, "Yes, Lord, yet even the dogs eat the crumbs that fall from their masters' table." Then Jesus answered her, "O woman, great is your faith! Be it done for you as you desire." And her daughter was healed instantly. (Matthew 15:21–28)

"Persistence pays off" is a lovely phrase for a motivational poster, but let's be honest: to the parent of a three-year-old (or fifteen-year-old), persistence can translate as *annoying*. I remember chuckling over the message printed on a magnet posted on a friend's refrigerator: *Having children is like being pecked to death by ducks.* To say my friend had an active and persistent child would be an understatement. If you can relate, take hope, because persistence directed toward a positive course can indeed pay off! Persistence can be rewarding when it is directed toward helping children set goals and achieving objectives.

Parents with persistent children must also be persistent. We must be persistently patient! Matthew's Gospel offers an encounter Jesus had with a persistent mom during one of his journeys. She sought out Jesus to help her daughter who had a serious spiritual need. She first went to the disciples, but they saw her appeals as a nuisance. The rebuff from the disciples did not deter her. When she finally made it to Jesus, *she bowed down*.

Her posture speaks volumes! Matthew describes this woman as a Canaanite, which means she was a pagan foreign woman. Yet, she knelt down before Jesus in a show of respect. She was persistent, but she was not obnoxious—she was respectful. She was not the mom who would march into the school to bully the teacher to make sure her child receives preferential treatment. With nowhere else to turn and desperate to aid her child, she showed great faith by turning to the only One who could offer help.

Though at first glance Jesus seems indifferent and perhaps harsh in his response, it is in fact likely that he traveled an out-of-the-way route in order to encounter this woman.[39] In the process, he clarified the priority of Israel in his divine plan. This Gentile woman had greater faith than the Jews he came to deliver. She affirmed his identity, even as his own disciples struggled with acknowledging him as the Messiah. He reminded them of the main mission, while he recognized and acknowledged her great faith. The faith of the mother resulted in the healing of the daughter. Your faith as a parent is important. Do not hesitate to be a persistent parent when it comes to praying for your child.

### Respond

How persistent are you in prayer for your child? What are your greatest concerns for your child today?

### Prayer for the journey

Use your list of concerns as a prayer guide. Lord, along with these concerns, may my child respond to your persistent call. Amen.

# Waypoint 27

*You don't know what you ask*

> Then the mother of the sons of Zebedee came up to him with her sons, and kneeling before him she asked him for something. And he said to her, "What do you want?" She said to him, "Say that these two sons of mine are to sit, one at your right hand and one at your left, in your kingdom." Jesus answered, "You do not know what you are asking. Are you able to drink the cup that I am to drink?" They said to him, "We are able." He said to them, "You will drink my cup, but to sit at my right hand and at my left is not mine to grant, but it is for those for whom it has been prepared by my Father." And when the ten heard it, they were indignant at the two brothers. But Jesus called them to him and said, "You know that the rulers of the Gentiles lord it over them, and their great ones exercise authority over them. It shall not be so among you. But whoever would be great among you must be your servant, and whoever would be first among you must be your slave, even as the Son of Man came not to be served but to serve, and to give his life as a ransom for many." (Matthew 20:20–28)

## Reflect

Every parent wants the best for their children. I will be the first to admit I do not always know what is best. I recall praying about a specific job for one of my sons. I did not just pray—I PRAYED. The job was perfect for his interest, talent, and experience; surely, the Lord would see the facts and move on the powers that be to give him the job. When he did not get it, our family was devastated. But let me tell you the rest of the story. In less than a year, that division of the company went under. If the Lord had given us what we had prayed for, my son would have been out of a job.

I can identify with the mother who came to Jesus to ask him to employ her sons on his right and left. His response, "You don't know what you're asking" was not rude, but merciful. The mother's request was ambitious, but was also sincere. She wanted the best for her boys. I do not fault her for her desire—I get it!

The sons of this mom were two of the twelve disciples who had just heard Jesus tell them (in Matthew 19:28): "Truly, I say to you, in the new world, when the Son of Man will sit on his glorious throne, you who have followed me will also sit on twelve thrones, judging the twelve tribes of Israel." James, John, and their mother took the opportunity to ask Jesus to establish a special place for them. They did not realize the suffering that Jesus would have to go through, and the suffering that would be required of them as his followers. They "did not know what they were asking."[40]

My boys will never outgrow my wanting the best for them, but I recognize I must temper my parental desire for their good with trusting that God knows what is truly good and best for them. God has a plan for their lives, and I believe his plan is better than any dream I have for them. My constant prayer is that my children will achieve the goals God intended for their lives.

### Respond

In this passage, what quality did Jesus consider the greatest? How are you nurturing an attitude of service in your child?

### Prayer for the journey

Lord, I pray my child would develop a servant's heart. Help me to serve you and others in a way that honors you and influences my child. Amen.

# Waypoint 28

*The formula for a perfect child*

And they brought the boy to him. And when the spirit saw him, immediately it convulsed the boy, and he fell on the ground and rolled about, foaming at the mouth. And Jesus asked his father, "How long has this been happening to him?" And he said, "From childhood. And it has often cast him into fire and into water, to destroy him. But if you can do anything, have compassion on us and help us." And Jesus said to him, "'If you can'! All things are possible for one who believes." Immediately the father of the child cried out and said, "I believe; help my unbelief!" (Mark 9:20–24)

Reflect

When it comes to rearing children with strong religious convictions, I want a formula. You know what I mean: follow these simple steps and you will get a child who is compliant, godly, and *on fire* for Jesus. Is that too much to ask? Apparently it is, because there are no formulas.

Consider the desperate father who came to Jesus for help with his son who was under the influence of an evil spirit. As Jesus arrived on the scene, the Jewish experts argued about the best way to deal with the issue (Mark 9:14). The scribes had offered their formula for fixing the son, and the disciples offered theirs, but the formulas did not work and the child was still in need.[41]

Sister, the power of evil and the battle for the souls of our children is real. The battle is evident for this dad who cried out to Jesus in despair to help his child. I wonder if he raised his child to follow the tenets of faith. Did he do all the right things and check all the boxes of the Jewish law and evil still overcame his child? Now even the experts could not help. I can imagine the pain and fear the father felt over his child's frightening condition.

Can't you hear the emotion in the father's words to Jesus, "If you can, have compassion on us and help us!" Jesus carefully responded with a challenge, "If you can! All things are possible for one who believes." The father replied to Jesus with raw, transparent honesty, "I believe; help my unbelief."

Sometimes that is where I find myself as a parent. My faith is not perfect and I struggle to believe God will intervene on behalf of my children. I take comfort in knowing God understands the conflict of my faith. He not only understands my conflict, he understands each of my children and their struggles. The struggle of my faith shows my own desperate need for the mercy of God. This one thing I know: I must depend on him.

I wish I could write a formula that would guarantee godly, righteous children who will always turn from evil. The truth is, some children will readily do the right thing and others will test the waters or plunge right in when they should not. As a parent, there are no formulas; just faithfulness. I must be faithful to teach the principles of God's Word to my children. I must be faithful to pray those principles become truth in their lives as they walk out their own faith journey. I must also be faithful not only to teach, but also to live out the truth of God's Word in my life.

### Respond
How do the words of Jesus in Mark 9:23 give you courage to trust God to help you rear godly children? How are you modeling faithfulness to your children?

### Prayer for the journey
Lord, today I pray I will be faithful not only to teach your truth to my children, but also to live out the truth of your Word. Amen.

# Waypoint 29

*Mother-guilt*

"But when he came to himself, he said, 'How many of my father's hired servants have more than enough bread, but I perish here with hunger! I will arise and go to my father, and I will say to him, "Father, I have sinned against heaven and before you. I am no longer worthy to be called your son. Treat me as one of your hired servants."' And he arose and came to his father. But while he was still a long way off, his father saw him and felt compassion, and ran and embraced him and kissed him." (Luke 15:17–20)

Reflect

I set out to be a perfect parent, didn't you? Like you, I also purposed to have perfect children. Unfortunately, both my children and I missed the mark by a long shot. No seminar, book, or blog post could make them—or me—perfect.

The father in this famous parable (Luke 15:11–32) would have wanted perfect children too. Jesus told the story to show God's great love and mercy. Reading it as a parent, the parable offers much to teach us about being a parent of imperfect children.

We meet two sons. The younger son asked his father for his inheritance before the father died. Dad had to know this would not be in his son's best interest, yet he gave him the money. Why would he set him up for failure? My "control the situation, control the child" tendency has a hard time with the actions of this father. But I remember the times when I allowed my own children the space to fail and they learned some of their most significant life lessons. How many lessons did I keep from my children by manipulating circumstances and controlling situations?

Then there were the times when my children made mistakes and I used the "I told you so" guilt card. *Mother-guilt*—I know it well. But the father here did not use guilt. He waited patiently for the son to return. No doubt he prayed for mercy, and the son came to his senses and returned home.

When the father saw the son, he ran to meet him. The words depict joy and relief, but there is more to see here. In that culture, a father running would have been shameful. No self-respecting man would run, because to run he must hold up his tunic, which would bare his legs, and bare legs equaled humiliation![42] Why would a dad subject himself to such disgrace? He ran to reach his son before the boy entered the village. Otherwise, the villagers might meet his rebellious child with a ceremony called *kezazah*. In this ceremony, a large pot was broken in front of a child who attempted to return home. The people would shout, "You are now cut off from your people!" The entire village would reject the child. The father headed off this rejection and was willing to endure the shame to welcome his son home.[43]

The father took the shame and showed forgiveness and compassion. I need to remember this story when I want to throw the shame card! This is the love, mercy, and forgiveness God has shown me through Christ. How can I not offer the same to my child?

### Respond

Do you avoid guilt and shame in parenting your child? How do you see the actions of the father as being merciful and not an act of rescuing the son from consequences of his behavior?

### Prayer for the journey

Lord, thank you for your love and forgiveness. Help me to parent my child the same way. Help us all come to our senses and humble our hearts to repent. Amen.

# Waypoint 30

*Let the children come*

Read

And they were bringing children to him that he might touch them, and the disciples rebuked them. But when Jesus saw it, he was indignant and said to them, "Let the children come to me; do not hinder them, for to such belongs the kingdom of God. Truly, I say to you, whoever does not receive the kingdom of God like a child shall not enter it." And he took them in his arms and blessed them, laying his hands on them. (Mark 10:13–16)

Reflect

You may have heard the story about the mom with three rambunctious little boys. A friend asked her if she had it to do all over again would she have three children. She thought about it a moment, and responded, "Yes." She paused and then said, "Just not the same three."

If you are a parent, there have most likely been days when you felt the same way. I have done my share of complaining about my kids when they were irritable, rowdy, or uncooperative. No matter the age or stage, those days will come.

The accounts of Jesus with children are numerous throughout the Gospels. In Mark 10:13–16 we read of parents who traveled to bring their children to him so that he would touch and bless them. However, the disciples tried to keep these folks away from Jesus. Did they think children were a disruption or distraction? Did they believe children were not as important as adults? We do not know the disciples' true feelings about children, but we do know the feelings of Jesus toward them: He loved and welcomed them. He did not become exasperated with the children; he became exasperated with the disciples for their attitude. He ordered them to stop hindering the parents from bringing the children to him.[44]

We cannot fault the disciples too much, as they were following the custom of the day. The phrase, "seen and not heard," was in full force concerning children. Society kept them on the periphery until they became old enough to be useful.[45] Jesus went against the status quo and made himself available and attentive to the little ones. He valued them and honored them by using them to illustrate the type of faith needed to enter into heaven—faith like a child.

Our children are never too young to begin introducing them to Jesus. Military chapels and civilian churches have rituals to connect our children to their faith. These ceremonies are important events for children, families, and the faith community. What is most important for our children is that they do not just encounter the disciples and followers of Jesus, but that they have a personal encounter with Jesus. Jesus wants to bless our children, and the greatest blessing they can receive from him is eternal life.

### Respond

How are you providing opportunities for your children to encounter Jesus? In what ways does your chapel or church make children welcome?

### Prayer for the journey

Lord, help me to see my children as a blessing and not a burden. I pray they would know and never doubt their value to our family. I pray they would know and never doubt their value to you. Amen.

# Notes for Journey 1

1. Richard Bowyer, *Dictionary of Military Terms* (Chicago, IL: Fitzroy Dearborn Publishers, 1999), 28.

2. Raymond Monsur Scurfield, Katherine Theresa Platoni, *War Trauma and Its Wake: Expanding the Circle of Healing* (New York: Routledge, 2013), 269.

3. Bruce Waltke, *Genesis* (Grand Rapids: Zondervan, 2001), 88.

4. John E. Hartley, *Genesis: Understanding the Bible Commentary Series* (Grand Rapids: Baker Books, 2000), 61.

5. NET Bible Notes, https://net.bible.org/#!bible/Genesis+2:18, accessed 4/24/15.

6. Gordon J. Wenham, *Word Biblical Commentary: Genesis 1–15* (Nashville: Thomas Nelson, 1987), 69.

7. NET Notes on Genesis 2:24; https://lumina.bible.org/bible/Genesis+2, accessed 4/27/15.

8. Claus Westermann *Genesis 1–11* (Minneapolis: Augsburg Press, 1984), 234.

9. Westermann, 235.

10. Wenham, 72.

11. NET Notes, https://lumina.bible.org/bible/Genesis+2, accessed April 28, 2015.

12. Waltke, 90.

13. Walter Brueggemann, *Genesis: A Bible Commentary for Teaching and Preaching* (Louisville: John Knox Press, 2010), 51.

14. George MacDonald, *St. George and St. Michael* (London: Keagan Paul, 1878), 258.

15. John Gottman, *The Science of Trust* (New York: W. W. Norton & Company, 2011), 178.

16. Matt Woodley, *The Gospel of Matthew, God with Us* (Downers Grove, IL: InterVarsity Press, 2011), 31.

17. Donald A. Hagner, *Word Biblical Commentary: Matthew 1–13* (Dallas: Word, Inc, 1993), 18.

18. Julia Plaff, "A Team Approach to Military Life" *Military.com*, http://www.military.com/spouse/relationships/military-marriage/team-approach-to-military-life.html, accessed May 10, 2015.

19. Thomas C. Wyatt and Reuven Gal, ed., *Legitimacy and Commitment in the Military* (Westport, CT: Greenwood Press, 1990), 183.

20. Sara Horn, "Keeping Your Guard/Reserve Marriage Strong," *Military.com*, http://www.military.com/spouse/relationships/military-marriage/keeping-strong-guard-reserve-marriage.html, accessed May 12, 2015.

21. John Nolland, *Word Biblical Commentary: Luke 1–9:20* (Dallas: Word Books, 1989), 104.

22. LA Times Religious News Service, "A Long, Cold Road to Bethlehem," *LA Times*, December 23, 1995, http://articles.latimes.com/1995-12-23/local/me-17102_1_gospel-accounts, accessed May 15, 2015.

23. Ibid.

24. Brené Brown, *Daring Greatly* (New York: Gotham Books, 2012), 53.

25. Richard L. Strauss, "Do You Trust Me? The Story of Mary and Joseph," https://bible.org/seriespage/ 11-do-you-trust-me-story-joseph-and-mary, accessed May 9, 2015.

26. *IVP Women's Bible Commentary*, 16.

27. Dorothee Soelle, Katharina Elliger, *Great Couples of the Bible* (Minneapolis, MN: Augsburg Fortress Press, 2006), 50.

28. Bill T. Arnold, *The New Cambridge Bible Commentary: Genesis* (New York: Cambridge University Press, 2009), 231.

29. Robert Alter, *Genesis: Translation and Commentary* (New York: W.W. Norton & Company, 1996), 128.

30. Paul Herring, "Isaac and Rebekah: A Failure to Communicate," Global Truth International, http://globaltruthinternational.com/2012/11/15/isaac-and-rebekah-a-failure-to-communicate/, accessed May 20, 2015.

31. Bruce K. Waltke, *Genesis* (Grand Rapids, MI: Zondervan, 2001), 358.

32. *IVP Women's Bible Commentary*, 17.

33. Chief Rabbi Lord Sacks, "The Tragedy of Good Intentions: Genesis 25:19–28:9," *Covenant & Conversation*, http://www.aish.com/tp/i/sacks/134230588.html, accessed May 17, 2015.

34. Gary Chapman and Jocelyn Green, *The Five Love Languages: Military Edition* (Chicago: Northfield Publishing, 2013).

35. Andrew Theen, "Oregon's 'Military Mistress,' Wanted for Check Fraud," *The Oregonian/Oregon Live*, April 7, 2015. http://www.oregonlive.com/pacific-northwest-news/index.ssf/2015/04/oregons_military_mistress_who.html, accessed May 16, 2015.

36. Arnold, 245.

37. Arnold, 247.

38. Jessica N. Modrell, "Relationship Maintenance of Military Couples" 8-1-2014. Doctor of Psychology (PsyD) program at George Fox University, Thesis and Dissertation. http://digitalcommons.georgefox.edu/cgi/viewcontent.cgi?article=1154&context=psyd, 46, accessed May 18, 2015.

39. Randy Fujishin, *Creating Communication: Exploring and Expanding Your Fundamental Communication Skills* (Lanham, MD: Rowman & Littlefield Publishers, 2009), 42.

40. Gary and Barbara Rosberg, *Divorce-Proof Your Marriage* (Nashville, TN: Tyndale House, 2002), 136.

41. Hara Estroff Marano, "Marriage Math," *www.psychologytoday.com*, March 16, 2004. https://www.psychologytoday.com/articles/200403/marriage-math. Accessed May 18, 2015.

42. Waltke, 404.

43. Rebecca Tews-Kozlowski and Desirée King, *Handbook of Counseling Military Couples* (New York: Routledge Taylor & Francis Group, 2012), 338.

44. Waltke, 405.

45. Arnold, 267.

46. David and Claudia Arp, John and Margaret Bell, *Loving Your Relatives: Even When You Don't See Eye-to-Eye* (Colorado Springs: Focus on the Family, 2003), 50.

47. Jens Manuel Krogstad, "5 Facts about the Modern American Family," www.pewresearch.org, April 30, 2014. http://www.pewresearch.org/fact-tank/2014/04/30/5-facts-about-the-modern-american-family/ accessed May 20, 2015.

48. "Tools for Ministering to Military Stepfamilies," www.militaryready-family.org http://militaryreadyfamily.org/ministering-to-stepfamilies.html, accessed May 20, 2015.

49. "Blended Families and the Military," www.militaryreadyfamily.org http://militaryreadyfamily.org/blended-families.html accessed May 20, 2015.

50. Waltke, 415.

51. Walter Brueggemann, *Genesis* (Louisville, KY: Westminster John Knox Press, 1982), 253.

52. *The IVP Women's Bible Commentary*, 22–23.

53. Paul Borgman, *Genesis: The Story We Haven't Heard* (Downers Grove, IL: InterVarsity Press, 2001), 166.

54. John H. Walton, *The NIV Application Commentary: Genesis* (Grand Rapids, MI: Zondervan, 2001), 592.

55. James McKeown, *The Two Horizons Old Testament Commentary: Genesis* (Grand Rapids, MI: Wm. B. Eerdmans, 2008), 152.

56. Dorothy Kelley Patterson and Rhonda Harrington Kelley, editors, *Women's Evangelical Commentary: Old Testament* (Nashville, TN: B&H Publishing, 2011), 77.

57. Carol A. Newsom, Sharon H. Ringe, Jacqueline E. Lapsley, editors, *Women's Bible Commentary* (Louisville, KY: Westminster John Knox Press, third edition, 2012), 241.

58. Bob Deffenbaugh, "The Way of the Wise: Studies in the Book of Proverbs: A Model for Marriage," www.bible.org, https://bible.org/seriespage/13-model-marriage, accessed May 21, 2015.

59. Christine R. Yoder, *Abingdon Old Testament Commentaries: Proverbs* (Nashville, TN: Abingdon Press, 2009), 292.

60. Yoder, 293.

61. Huffington Post, "Happy Marriages Require Generosity," 12/16/2011, http://www.huffingtonpost.com/2011/12/16/happy-marriages_n_1152080.html, accessed May 22, 2015.

62. W. Bradford Wilcox, "Does Marital Generosity Flow Outward?" January 28, 2011, http://blogs.nd.edu/science-of-generosity/2011/01/28/does-marital-generosity-flow-outward/#more-663, accessed May 23, 2015.

63. Duane A. Garrett, Proverbs, *The New American Commentary: Ecclesiastes, Song of Songs, Vol. 14* (Nashville, TN: B&H Publishing Group, 1993), 250.

64. Gary Chapman, *Things I Wish I'd Known Before We Got Married* (Chicago, IL: Northfield Publishing, 2010), 81.

65. Elmer Towns, *How to Build a Lasting Marriage: Lessons from Bible Couples* (Shippensburg, PA: Destiny Image, 2003), 70.

66. Luke uses Priscilla as a nickname for the formal Prisca.

67. Herbert Lockyer, *All the Women of the Bible* (Grand Rapids, MI: Zondervan, 1967), 122.

68. Marie Noel Keller, *Priscilla and Aquila: Paul's Coworkers in Christ Jesus* (Collegeville, MN: Liturgical Press, 2010), xv.

69. R. Paul & Gail Stevens, *Marriage: Learning from Couples in Scripture* (Colorado Springs, CO: WaterBrook Press, 2005), 89.

# Notes for Journey 2

1.  Bruce Waltke, *Genesis: A Commentary* (Grand Rapids, MI: Zondervan, 2001), 55.

2.  Carolyn Custis James, *Lost Women of the Bible* (Grand Rapids, MI: Zondervan, 2005), 54.

3.  Victor Hamilton, *The New International Commentary on the Old Testament: Genesis 1–17* (Grand Rapids, MI: Wm. B. Eerdmans, 1990), 273–274.

4.  Matthew A. Carlyle, "Sticking Together: A Military Family Story," www.navy.mil 4/30/2014. http://www.navy.mil/submit/display. asp?story_id=80712 (accessed June 3, 2015).

5.  Ibid.

6.  Waltke, 137.

7.  Kariah Church, "Perfect Parents…?" *Military Spouse Forum*, April 3, 2015. http://community.militaryspouse.com/threads/perfect-parents.1600/ (accessed June 3, 2015).

8.  Waltke 155.

9.  Pew Research Center. "The Military-Civilian Gap: Fewer Family Connections," November 23, 2011, http://www.pewsocialtrends. org/2011/11/23/the-military-civilian-gap-fewer-family-connections/ (accessed June 3, 2015).

10. http://www.militarychild.org/student-identifier (accessed June 3, 2015).

11. Dorothy Kelly Peterson and Rhonda Kelly, editors, *Women's Evangelical Commentary: Old Testament* (Nashville, TN: Holman Reference, 2011), 113.

12. Jewish Virtual Library, "Jewish Victims of the Holocaust: Hidden Children," https://www.jewishvirtuallibrary.org/jsource/Holocaust/ hidden.html (accessed June 6, 2015).

13. Bloeme Evers-Emden, "Hiding Jewish Children during World War II: The Psychological Aftermath," *Jewish Political Studies Review* (March 2007), Jerusalem Center for Public Affairs, http://jcpa.org/article/

hiding-jewish-children-during-world-war-ii-the-psychological-aftermath/ (accessed June 6, 2015).

14. Steven J. Cole, "Lesson 18: Stephen-the Message (Acts 7:1–53)," https://bible.org/seriespage/lesson-18-stephen-message-acts-71-53 (accessed June 6, 2015).

15. Kenneth Boa, "Perspectives on Parenthood," https://bible.org/article/perspectives-parenthood (accessed June 6, 2015).

16. Douglas K. Stuart, *Exodus: An Exegetical and Theological Exposition of Holy Scripture* (Nashville, TN: Broadman & Holman, 2006), 88.

17. John Phillips, *Exploring People of the Old Testament* (Grand Rapids, MI: Kregel Academic Publishers, 2006), 218.

18. Randall C. Bailey, *The College Press NIV Commentary: Exodus* (Collegedale, TN: College Press Publishing Co, 2007), 73.

19. Amy Bushatz, "Have You Met a MilSpouse Bully?" www.spousebuzz.com FRG/Spouse Support, August 20, 2012, http://spousebuzz.com/blog/2012/08/have-you-met-a-milspouse-bully.html (accessed June 11, 2015).

20. Rosiland Wiseman, *Queen Bee Moms & Kingpin Dads* (New York: Three Rivers Press, 2006), 6.

21. Deuteronomy 12:17–18 provides guidelines for the festival.

22. Temper Longman III and David Garland, *The Expositor's Bible Commentary: 1 Samuel-2 Kings* (Grand Rapids, MI: Zondervan, 2010), 47.

23. Edward E. Hindson, Daniel R. Mitchell, *Zondervan King James Version Commentary: Old Testament* (Grand Rapids, MI: Zondervan, 2010), 367.

24. Longman & Garland, 48.

25. Trevor Dennis, *Sarah Laughed* (Nashville, TN: Abingdon Press, 1994), 124.

26. Custis James, 135.

27. Blue Star Mothers of America, Inc, http://www.bluestarmothers.org (accessed July 1, 2015).

28. Catherine Clark Kroeger and Mary J. Evans, *The IVP Women's Bible Commentary* (Downers Grove, ILL: InterVarsity Press, 2002), 564.

29. F. Scott Spencer, *Salty Wives, Spirited Mothers, and Savvy Widows* (Grand Rapids, MI: Wm B. Eerdmans, 2012), 84.

30. Ibid.

31. Darrell Bock, *Baker Exegetical Commentary of the New Testament: Luke 1:1–9:50* (Grand Rapids, MI: Baker Publishing Group, 1994) 235.

32. Williamsburg Military Insider, "Military BRAT ... Do You Know the True Meaning?" http://williamsburgmilitaryinsider.com/2011/04/14/military-brat-do-you-know-the-true-meaning/ (accessed July 7, 2015).

33. Bock, 263.

34. Ibid, 264.

35. Gary M. Burge, *The NIV Application Commentary: Gospel of John* (Grand Rapids, MI: Zondervan, 2000), 41.

36. Dawn Risas, "The Lost Ones," Military Brat Life: Celebrating Our Unique Culture. http://www.militarybratlife.com/articles/the-lost-ones.html (accessed July 7, 2015).

37. Grant R. Osborne and Clinton E. Arnold, *Exegetical Commentary of the New Testament: Matthew* (Grand Rapids, MI: Zondervan), 552.

38. Craig S. Keener, *Acts: An Exegetical Commentary, Volume 1* (Grand Rapids, MI: Baker Books, 2012), 674.

39. Krueger and Evans, 534.

40. Craig S. Keener, *The IVP New Testament Commentary Series: Matthew* (Downers Grove, ILL: InterVarsity Press, 1997), 308.

41. R. Kent Hughes, *Mark: Jesus, Servant and Savior, Volume 2* (Winchester, ILL: Crossway Books, 1989), 34.

42. Matt Williams, "The Prodigal Son's Father Shouldn't Have Run!: Putting Luke 15:11–32 in Context" *Biola Magazine*, Summer 2010. http://magazine.biola.edu/article/10-summer/the-prodigal-sons-father-shouldnt-have-run/ (accessed July 17, 2015).

43. Ibid.

44. Robert H. Stein, *Baker Exegetical Commentary on the New Testament: Mark* (Grand Rapids, MI: Baker Academic, 2008), 463.

45. Bock, 298.